MARXIST–HUMANISM
IN THE PRESENT MOMENT

Marxist-Humanism in the Present Moment

Reflections on Theory and Practice in Light of the Covid-19 Pandemic and the Black Lives Matter Uprisings

Edited by

Jens Johansson and Kristopher Baumgartner

ISBN: 978-1-7368804-0-1

International Marxist-Humanist Organization
PO Box 60391
Suite 900
Chicago, IL 60660

arise@imhojournal.org

Typesetting & composition by Kristopher Baumgartner
Cover illustration by Damian Algabre

Contents

Notes on Authors

The Steering Committee of the IMHO is a democratically elected committee within the IMHO, which has the coordinating responsibility of the organization when not in Convention.

Peter Hudis has written widely on Marxist theory and contemporary politics and is the author of Marx's Concept of the Alternative to Capitalism, and Frantz Fanon: Philosopher on the Barricades. He is General Editor of The Complete Works of Rosa Luxemburg (three volumes have appeared so far).

Rhaysa Ruas is a young Afro-Brazilian attorney, researcher, and social activist based in Rio de Janeiro.

Ndindi Kitonga is a Kenyan-American revolutionary educator and a long-time organizer and activist in Los Angeles who has written on revolutionary critical pedagogy and democratic education.

Heather A. Brown has written widely on Marxism, feminism, and ecology and is the author of Marx on Gender and the Family.

Kevin B. Anderson has authored Marx at the Margins: On Nationalism, Ethnicity, and Non-Western Societies and Lenin, Hegel, and Western Marxism. Among his edited books are The Power of Negativity by Raya Dunayevskaya (with Peter Hudis), Karl Marx (with Bertell Ollman), The Rosa Luxemburg Reader (with Peter Hudis), and The Dunayevskaya-Marcuse-Fromm Correspondence (with Russell Rockwell).

Seamus Connolly is a writer on humanism and Marxism.

Jens Johansson is a former mineworker and a student activist in Sweden.

Lilia D. Monzó uses Marxist-Humanist and decolonial approaches to confront capitalism and imperialism, racism, and the hyper-exploitation of women of color, while envisioning a socialist alternative. She is the author of A Revolutionary Subject: Pedagogy of Women of Color and Indigeneity.

Karel Ludenhoff is an Amsterdam-based labor activist and a writer on Marx's critique of political economy whose essays have appeared in Logos and other journals.

Foreword

Since its founding in 2009, the activities of the International Marxist-Humanist Organization have been guided by the aim of developing and projecting a viable alternative to capitalism – a new human society – that can give direction to today's freedom struggles. As members of the IMHO, we find inspiration for working out what a humanist alternative to capitalism means from a specific body of thought, that of Karl Marx and also that of Marxist-Humanism, as it was first worked out by Raya Dunayevskaya in the 1950s and later developed by numerous activists and scholars in the Marxist-Humanist tradition. The fact that the IMHO bases itself in a specific body of thought makes us a particular type leftwing organization today. Few other political organizations take up the task of unifying philosophy and organization, and theory and practice, as seriously as we in the IMHO do.

That the IMHO has clearly expressed philosophic grounding in the tradition of Marxist-Humanism does not mean that we have a fixed set of ideas that never changes, or that we only repeat conclusions that were worked out long time ago. Instead, we hold that each generation must work out what Marx's Marxism means for today. As Dunayevskaya once wrote: "Marx's legacy is no mere heirloom, but a live body of ideas and perspectives that is in need of concretization. Every moment of Marx's development, as well as the totality of his works, spells out the need for 'revolution in permanence.' This is the absolute challenge to our age." This year, 2020, the creativity of the masses in the anti-racist protests around the world that took off after the tragic killing of Mr. George Floyd in Minneapolis, Breonna Taylor in Louisville, and so many others, has shown us new aspects of what it means to unite theory and practice. In the IMHO we have worked hard to analyze, contextualize, and influence this movement, as well as also acknowledging the need for ourselves to be influenced from and to learn from it, especially from the opportunities it sees and the challenges it faces.

Part of the project of developing a viable alternative to capitalism and giving direction to today's freedom movements is to reach out with the thoughts that we develop. This publication is a collection of presentations given at our 2020 Convention, which this year had to be held online due to the global pandemic. For two days in July, members of the IMHO came together and discussed political and theoretical issues and decided upon future activities of the organization. The IMHO is an international organization, and we have members from all over the world who are involved in lots of different struggles which had different perspectives to add to our conversation. We had seven presentations during the convention, which we think summarized important issues and caught significant ideas about the concretization of Marx's Marxism for today.

In this book, we publish these presentations from our Convention in a form slightly edited to fit the printed format. We have also added our Call to the Convention, which was written in April as part of the pre-Convention discussions.

These presentations cover a wide range of topics. Rhaysa Ruas's report takes its starting point in Brazil and the developments there since Bolsonaro was elected. Ndindi Kitonga reports directly from this year's Black Lives Matter demonstrations, and Heather A. Brown discusses the ecological crisis, Kevin B Anderson takes up Covid-19 and capitalism, Peter Hudis unpacks Frantz Fanon's thought in light of today's movements, and Seamus Connolly defends the concept of humanism from postmodern attacks.

A red thread that runs through all the presentations is that human life under capitalism gets treated as a means toward an end rather than as an end in itself. Under capitalism, the abstraction value mediates human relations and hinders us from relating to each other in a truly human way. Instead, the augmentation of value becomes an end in itself, and under this system human beings and human relations gets subsumed. In our Constitution we write: "An alternative to capitalism means ending production for value, creating a humanist mode of production, establishing a new non-state form of governance, and building freely associated human relations. Breaking with the law of value is the necessary condition for the possibility of the formation of a truly new society, as value production subordinates human beings to things and distorts human relations." This notion is key to the Marxist–Humanist tradition and is the reason why some of the presentations go into a direct discussion on what it means to uproot capitalism and to establish a system in which human life on a systematic level gets treated as a nothing else but as an end in itself.

If you as a reader of this book find the presentations resonating with your own ideas or experiences, we would appreciate it very much if you would write to us and tell us about it. Our email address is arise@imhojournal.org, and we always try to respond to all emails we receive as quickly as possible. Also, if you would like to get to know more about or to get involved in the IMHO, please send us an email or come to one of our events. As of now, December 2020, the Covid-19 pandemic is still spreading rapidly over the world, and until it is safe again to meet physically, all our events will be held online. Information about upcoming events is announced on our webpage www.imhojournal.org.

The preparation and editing of this publication was done mainly by Kristopher Baumgartner and Jens Johansson, with a cover design by Damian Algabre. On behalf of the whole organization, we hope that you as a reader will find the texts as stimulating and thought-provoking as we have, and we sincerely invite you to take part in discussing them.

— Jens Johansson, Communication and Outreach Coordinator of the IMHO
December 2020, Malmö, Sweden

Chapter 1

Where to Begin? Growing Seeds of Liberation in a World Torn Asunder

By *the* Steering Committee of the International Marxist-Humanist Organization

What faces us in the post-COVID-19 world as we struggle to uproot capitalism and its malignant racism, sexism, heterosexism, and environmental destruction, both in theory and in practice. Authored by Peter Hudis, with Kevin B. Anderson, Karel Ludenhoff, Lilia D. Monzó, and Jens Johansson as part of the pre-Convention discussion of the International Marxist-Humanist Organization.

> *It never fails that, at momentous world historic turning points, it is very difficult to tell the difference between two types of twilight—whether one is first plunging into utter darkness or whether one has reached the end of a long night and is just at the moment before the dawn of a new day. In either case, the challenge to find the meaning—what Hegel called "the undefined foreboding of something unknown"—becomes a compulsion to dig for new beginnings, for a philosophy that would try to answer the question, "where to begin"?*

> —Raya Dunayevskaya, "Why Hegel's *Phenomenology*? Why Now?"

I

The shock that has been delivered to global politics and economics by the spread of the coronavirus clearly places us on the edge of a precipice. The economic "recovery" that was touted only months ago in the U.S. and elsewhere has been rendered hollow by a contraction in the global economy greater than in a century, while the political instability that has defined world politics for the last decade is becoming increasingly acute. The Chinese government's effort to conceal the extent of the virus is matched only by the willful ignorance and inhumanity of the Trump administration, which has shown itself to be more intent on blaming "foreigners"—and everyone but itself—for the illness than providing adequate testing and treatment. The breakdown in commerce, schooling, international travel and social interaction of all kinds in the face of efforts to contain the contagion may prove to be temporary expedients, but they also reveal the fragility of the social and human connections that are supposed to bind us together.

A striking sign of this is the lack of international coordination in combatting the pandemic, despite the fact that fifteen years ago the World Health Organization (WHO) revised its International Health Regulations by creating a series of regulations aimed at responding to exactly the kind of pandemic now facing us. Although almost every country in the world signed onto the new regulations, few have followed them—including the U.S., which ignored the requirement to inform the WHO before imposing quarantines and travel bans. The "globally interconnected world" promised by neoliberal capitalism is increasingly illusory.

Most importantly, the pandemic is expanding the divide between the "two worlds" within each country, between rulers and ruled, haves and have-nots, the privileged and the dispossessed. Tens of millions who have lost their jobs due to quarantines and physical distancing are without the means to pay rent, purchase food, or obtain the healthcare needed to deal with the crisis. In the U.S., the most vulnerable include undocumented immigrants, among them two-and-a-half million agricultural laborers, who are denied access to government assistance; prisoners, whose infection rates are skyrocketing; and those confined to nursing homes and assisted living facilities. The pandemic is amplifying not only the class but also racial divide that has long defined capitalist societies; 70% of those who have so far died from COVID-19 in Chicago are African American.

U.S. healthcare workers are being subjected to serious risks—both medical and social. Utah's largest medical provider, Intermountain Health Care, is cutting salaries of doctors and nurses on grounds that it needs "flexibility" in dealing with the crisis. The corporate bottom line always matters more than human life. Meanwhile, hundreds of billions of dollars have been pumped into international financial markets by the Federal Reserve and the European Central Bank to aid corporations that spent the last decade handsomely rewarding their shareholders with stock buybacks. To give but one of many such examples, thousands of workers at airports on the East Coast were told without warning by their employer, OTG, that they were being terminated on the spot in March without severance pay and had to leave the premises immediately. Some had worked for OTG for thirty years. When the workers complained of their callous mistreatment, they were told to ask for assistance from local governments. Yet this very same OTG will be on the receiving end of billions of dollars now being doled out by the federal government's $2 trillion-plus "economic stabilization plan" that became law on March 26.

That plan does provide for an extension of unemployment benefits and a modest cash payment of $1,200 for individuals making less than $75,000 a year. But the vast bulk of the money will be used to enable the Federal Reserve to buy up U.S. Treasury and other bonds as a way to prevent a collapse of the international financial system. This sounds like a repeat of 2007-2008, when trillions were spent propping up the banks while virtually nothing was done for homeowners facing foreclosure and workers being laid off. Yet the current bailout is in many respects even more egregious, since "The Fed will effectively lend money directly to large corporations, *something it has never done before.*" [1]

Meanwhile, Trump has been reluctant to issue *national* guidelines requiring social distancing—the only known way of controlling the spread of the virus—since he apparently views the careening stock market as a greater danger than tens of thousands of deaths. Small wonder that on February 10, almost a month after the first case of coronavirus was reported in the U.S., he submitted a 2021 budget that called for a $693 million *reduction* in funding for the Centers for Disease Control and Prevention—a cut of 9%. Clearly, the crisis surrounding the coronavirus has laid bare the social contradictions

---

1. Jeanna Smialek, "The Fed Plans to Do Whatever It Takes, and More than It Ever Has," *The New York Times*, March 24, 2020, pp. B4-5.

that define American and *world* capitalism.

This crisis is not only political and economic, but also *ideological*. And it impacts leftists as well. The Italian philosopher Giorgio Agamben, seen by some as a successor to Michel Foucault, recently criticized what he calls "the frenetic, irrational and entirely unfounded emergency measures adopted against an alleged epidemic of coronavirus." He asks, "Why do the media and the authorities do their utmost to spread a state of panic, thus provoking an authentic state of exception with serious limitations on movement and a suspension of daily life in entire regions?" He condemns the measures to combat the virus as "once again manifesting the tendency to use a state of exception as a normal paradigm for government...the disproportionate reaction to something not too different from the normal flu that affects us every year is quite blatant. It is almost as if with terrorism exhausted as a cause for exceptional measures, the invention of an epidemic offered the ideal pretext for scaling them up beyond any limitation."[2] Trump would have us die for the sake of the stock market; Agamben would so do for the sale of his theory of "the state of exemption." Such is the ideological pollution of our times.

II

Of course, the roots of our current crisis long predate the coronavirus. Thrown into disarray by the 2008 global financial meltdown, neoliberalism is increasingly being disavowed around the world—including by some of the agents of capital, who have decided to drop the veneer of "democracy" and "civil society" by openly embracing xenophobic nationalism, protectionism, and unabashed authoritarianism. This is seen from the rise of the neo-fascist Right in Europe and the fascistic policies of Modi in India, to Russia's Putin, Turkey's Erdogan, and China's Xi Jinping's grab for permanent one-man rule and the racist and misogynist rule of

---

2. Agamben, Georgio "The Invention of an Epidemic" in *Quodlibet*, February 26, 2020. Accessible here: https://www.quodlibet.it/giorgio-agamben-1-invenzione-di-un-epidemia

Brazil's Bolsonaro. The more social relations become indirect and frayed by capitalist alienation, the greater is the drive by state powers to impose direct social control over recalcitrant parts of the populace. This is becoming even further accentuated by rulers worldwide who are using the restrictions needed to contain COVID-19 to further cement unilateral, authoritarian rule—by closing borders, increasing government surveillance, restricting free expression, etc.

Yet as dire as all this is, we must not lose sight of the fact that the past year has experienced a remarkable upsurge in mass protests and revolts. They include spontaneous movements in Sudan, Algeria, and Lebanon, the first of which brought down its government; large protests and strikes against economic austerity in France, Chile, Ecuador, Colombia, Iran, Iraq, Zimbabwe, and Indonesia; and a massive pro-democracy movement in Hong Kong that involved up to two million at a time. The movement in Chile typifies what characterizes many of them. It began with high school students jumping turnstiles in response to a hike in subway fares, and was soon followed by hundreds of thousands pouring into the streets to support them. When President Sebastian Piñera tried to suppress the protests, people responded by creating citizen assemblies. Dozens of these decentralized, highly democratic forums have sprung up in Santiago and elsewhere in the country, involving men and women, workers and the unemployed, gays and straights, Mapuche Indians as well as immigrants from Brazil, Haiti, and elsewhere. They have maintained these assemblies for months in pressing for a fundamental change of society.

One report stated, "Just as during Argentina's crisis in 2001, neighbors are meeting to comment about their reality and take concrete measures against the repressive model" embodied by the government. One participant in the assemblies explained the moment as follows: "We are living a total break with the everyday life to which we were subjected. That's why the atmosphere is very special, invigorating and very joyful. We are recovering a sense of humanity from the rebellion, the appropriation of spaces in our communities."[3]

---

3. Quoted in Boccacci, Juan Manuel "Citizen Assemblies Are Challenging the Neoliberal Model in Chile" in *Orinoco Tribune*, February 3, 2020.

Identical sentiments can be heard from many other movements of the past year. What drives them is anxiety over mounting personal debt, growing social inequality, environmental destruction, and a sense that everyday life is losing any connection to a common space in which to share ideas and values. As Carne Ross, the author of *The Leaderless Revolution: How Ordinary People Will Take Power and Change Politics in the 21st Century*, states, these revolts "all represent a crisis of agency—of people who feel unrepresented. For that reason, philosophically, they tend to not be top-down movements. If people want their own voice, they're not happy if someone stands up and says they represent you. 'We represent ourselves' is a common feature of these protests."[4]

Virtually all of these struggles have been halted for now by the restrictions imposed to stem the spread of the coronavirus. But that does not mean they are ancient history. This crisis is so rapidly tearing the veil from illusions that capitalism is a viable system that it is implausible to believe that things will return to "normal" once the epidemic recedes. Consciousness of the need to supplant this system by a totally different one is bound to grow and develop, for which the struggles and movements of the past year have already planted many seeds.

No such mass revolts have occurred recently in the U.S., although the same seeds of radical self-organized liberation have grown within numerous grassroots movements, from Standing Rock to tenant organizing and mutual-aid during the COVID-19 crisis. Yet something no less important has emerged—growing interest, especially among youth, in the idea of socialism. The roots of this remarkable burst of interest lie in the Occupy Movement of 2011, but it gained a powerful impetus with the presidential campaign of Bernie Sanders. More people in the U.S. today openly identify with socialism than in many decades. To be sure, much of this interest is superficial and undeveloped; when it comes to Sanders, it is largely defined by the call for a "New Deal Workers' Bill of Rights" that

---

4. Wright, Robin "The Story of 2019: Protests in Every Corner of the Globe" in *The New Yorker*, December 30, 2019.

Roosevelt championed in his last inaugural address in 1944.[5] But that is not the crucial issue. The crucial issue is that the idea of socialism is at least becoming part of public discourse, which makes it possible to develop an open, ongoing discussion and debate that takes the idea further than presently articulated.

This was precisely the development that scared the Democratic Party establishment into rallying around Biden—one of the weakest candidates in the field and much further to the Right than not only Sanders but also Elizabeth Warren. Nothing is more alarming for those who imagine that the neoliberal order that dominated the last 40 years can readily be restored than the growing attraction of socialist ideas. At the same time, the primaries show that there is a long way to go before even the moderate socialism of Sanders is widely accepted, as seen in the lack of a high turnout for him, especially among women and Black voters—due at least in part to Sanders' lack of a sufficiently close engagement with those sectors.

Nevertheless, despite his limitations, Sanders won a plurality of the under-35 vote in *every* demographic—Black, Latinx and white, women and men, working class and middle class. This did not translate into many primary victories, largely because there wasn't a high turnout of young voters and the over-50 vote went overwhelmingly for Biden. But even the low turnout among youth is reflective in some cases of a radicalized social consciousness: as Deonte Washington, a Black youth who served 18 months in Florida (including part in solitary confinement)—and then had his voting rights restored by the 2018 referendum—put it, "I'm not going to vote, I don't care about this government and this government doesn't care about me."[6]

Revolutionary opponents of capitalism clearly have their work cut out for them. But as the young Marx wrote, we do not confront

---

5. Sanders addresses his debt to FDR's speech in "What Democratic Socialism Means Today," in *An Inheritance for Our Times: The Principles and Politics of Democratic Socialism*, edited by Gregory Smulewicz-Zucker and Michael J. Thompson (New York and London: OR Books, 2020).

6. Casey, Richard "Does Florida Really Want Ex-Felons to Vote?" in *The New York Times*, March 17, 2020.

today's realities "in a doctrinaire way with a new principle: Here is the truth, kneel down before it! We develop new principles for the world out of the world's own principles. We do not say to the world: Cease your struggles, they are foolish; we will give you the true slogan of struggle. We merely show the world what it is really fighting for, and consciousness is something that it *has* to acquire, even if it does not want to."[7]

The International Marxist-Humanist Organization has an important role to play in developing *conscious* awareness of a genuine alternative to existing society, since the body of ideas of Marxist-Humanism contains critical historical and theoretical resources that can illuminate both the logic of capital and the content of a socialist alternative that transcends the failed variants which dominated in the past. Integral to this is its view that racism and sexism are not secondary features of class society but are integral to capitalism's ability to reproduce itself in ever more nefarious forms. For this reason, the central theme of our 2020 Convention is not only the need for a viable alternative to capitalism but the *specific steps and practices* that we can embark upon in advancing one.

III

The effort to develop an alternative to capitalism always begins with the question, what is the *specific* nature of capitalism as it presents to us most immediately *today*?

The irrational exuberance with which Trump touted the economic "recovery" prior to the coronavirus crisis was expressed in a speech on December 16, 2017 which stated, "The economy now has hit 3% [growth per year]. Nobody thought we'd be anywhere close. I think we can go to 4, 5, and maybe even 6%." Yet as Michael Roberts writes, "Trump's boast turned to dust in 2019. U.S. GDP grew by 2.3% in 2019, well below President Trump's promise of 3% and more growth. The most recent GDP number proved that the tax cuts

---

7. Karl Marx, "Letter to Arnold Ruge" (September 1843), in *Marx-Engels Collected Works*, Vol. 3 (New York: International Publishers, 1975), p. 144.

championed by Trump had no sustained impact on U.S. growth...
Actually, cumulative growth under Trump has been lower than under
both Obama and Bush Jr."[8]

The lack of significant improvement in living standards helps
explain the 2019 strikes at General Motors, as well as the Chicago and
Los Angeles teachers strikes that won strong community support—
which focused not only on stagnant wages, but also conditions of labor
and the need for better services for students. The economic growth
that occurred prior to COVID-19 clearly was insufficient to reverse
growing social inequality. According to a recent report by OXFAM,
"The world's richest 1% have more than twice as much wealth as
6.9 billion people. Nearly half of the world's population—3.4 billion
people—is living on less than $5.50 a day. Every year, 100 million
people worldwide are pushed into poverty because they have to pay
out-of-pocket for healthcare. Today 258 million children—1 out of
every 5—will not be allowed to go to school. Globally, women earn
24% less than men and own 50% less wealth."[9]

Thomas Piketty's *Capital in the Twenty-First Century and Capital
and Ideology* confirm this tendency, but a confirmation is not an
explanation. To explain it, we have to turn to the mechanism of
capitalist production. Profit is generated in the process of production
through the creation of surplus value, which must be realized in
money. In order to realize more profit, the production process must
grow, and this cannot happen unless investment grows. However,
long before the coronavirus capital investment was falling in the
U.S. and elsewhere. The reason is not "changes in interest rates" or
in "business confidence," as many mainstream economists argue.
Those are usually the consequence, not the cause of, low demand. The
fundamental cause is profitability and the movement of corporate
profits. Evidence for that is in abundance. As Roberts writes, "the U.S.
rate of profit on productive capital remains well below where it was

---

8. Roberts, Michael "Trump's Trickle Dires Up" in *Michael Robert's Blog*,
February 2, 2020. Accessible here: https://thenextrecession.wordpress.
com/2020/02/04/trumps-trickle-dries-up/

9. Oxfam International. Accessible here: https://www.oxfam.org/en/what-we-
do/issues/extreme-inequality-and-essential-services

in the late 1990s. It was hardly boosted by the depreciation of assets in the 2008–2009 recession." This also applies to real GDP growth. "Growth is much lower than Trump hoped for because businesses have not invested productively but used the extra cash from tax cuts to pay larger dividends to shareholders; or buy back their own shares to boost the price; or to shift profits abroad into tax havens. They have not invested as much in new structures, equipment etc. in the U.S. because the profitability of such investments is still too low historically; and especially relative to investment in the 'fictitious capital' of the stock and bond markets, where prices have reached all-time highs."[10] Non-financial sector profits have fallen 25% since 2014! Although Trump's corporate tax cuts boosted post-tax profits, pre-tax profits continue to fall.

Low profitability in productive investments and the flight to fictitious capital is a global phenomenon. As Angela Klein writes, the global economic situation is akin to "dancing atop the volcano." She adds, "anything can happen in the current situation of declining production [in terms of] world trade and the financial markets; all it takes is a spark for the hut to burn again. This can easily be triggered by political decisions." Or by a virus? She writes, "The main problem is: there are no reserves left. This is all the more so since fundamental problems that led to the 2008 financial crisis have not been solved: global debt has reached a historic high—namely $250 trillion, which is three times as much as is produced in the world; according to the IMF, corporate debt, fueled by low interest rate policies, is higher than ever and surpasses the peaks of 2008–2009, 2001 and 1990, all of which were accompanied by recessions. The debts are held in the form of bonds on the capital market. If they have to be repaid at a higher interest rate in coming years, it will be expensive."[11]

This afflicts even the most "successful" capitalist enterprises, such as Amazon and Uber, which actually have yet to earn significant profits but get those with excess cash to throw money at them with promises of future rates of return. As Ross Douthat put it, "It has done all this

10. Roberts, Michael "Trump's Trickle Dires Up"

11. See Angela Klein, *Sozialistische Zeitung*, No. 4, 2019.

using the awesome power of free money, building a company that would collapse into bankruptcy if that money were withdrawn...The dearth of corporate investment also means that the steady climb of the stock market has boosted the wealth of a rentier class—basically, already rich investors getting richer off of dividends—rather than reflecting rising prosperity in general."[12] In a word, stagnation rules the day. This did not result from the coronavirus; that was instead its proximate cause. Capitalism has been producing a lot of rotten fruit that was just waiting to fall.

As a result, a sizeable section of the global ruling class is losing confidence that it can oversee a substantial improvement in the productive power of capital. Faced with internal barriers to increasing the size and rate of growth of capital accumulation, the elites are increasingly interested in looting the system of its assets so as to line their pockets before the next deluge. This is starkly expressed by such personages as Israel's Netanyahu, Britain's Boris Johnson, Brazil's Bolsonaro, and Trump. The lines that separate personal acquisitiveness from government have long been fuzzy, but at no time are they being erased at such a prodigious pace by an array of narcissistic politicians that are often labeled "rightwing populists."

Since today's growing inequality manifests what Marx called the law of the tendential fall of the rate of profit, the only solution is to create a human society that ends production based on value and surplus value. For that reason, the notion shared by both Piketty and socialists who focus on *redistributing* value can, at best, only bring some temporary improvement in the living conditions of working people but cannot end exploitation, alienation and dehumanization.

IV

Creating a new society requires masses of people aspiring to create one, which involves first of all listening to and learning from new developments coming from below. We are certainly not without such developments in the recent period.

---

12. Douthat, Ross "The Age of Decadence" in *The New York Times*, February 9, 2020.

The Middle East and North Africa have entered a new era in comparison with even a couple of years ago. As the organizers of a recent forum on "The Second Arab Spring" wrote, "in December 2018, a new uprising in Sudan inaugurated what has taken in 2019 the shape of a second revolutionary shockwave engulfing Algeria, Iraq and Lebanon, along with an outburst in Iran and tremors in Egypt. The second wave confirmed that the Arab Spring was but the first 'season' in a long-term revolutionary process."[13] Contrast this to even a couple years ago, when Egypt's military and the Saudi monarchy were riding high.

In Algeria, the Hirak movement immobilized the country for over a year, also bringing millions onto the streets. The Hirak put the regime on the defensive, but without achieving any major victories up to now. By the fall of 2019, the mass revolt had spread to Iraq and Lebanon, though not on the scale of Sudan or Algeria, with similar results to those in Algeria. Further east, Iran experienced a serious mass revolt in late 2019, which was ruthlessly repressed, after which the Trump administration threw the regime a lifeline by its illegal and reckless assassination of the popular military leader Qasem Soleimani.

A progressive development that inspired leftwing movements worldwide concerns the Kurdish forces of the People's Protection Units (YPG). The gender equality in the Kurdish forces, where women could be officers in mixed-gender units, not only helped defeat ISIS and laid the ground for the creation for the Kurdish Rojava enclave, but also freed thousands of Yazidi women from enslavement by ISIS at a time when the rest of the world stood by and did nothing. In their battle against ISIS, the YPG was backed by limited air support from U.S. forces. This gave Rojava and the Kurds a degree of protection from the Turkish regime, which views all struggles for Kurdish autonomy as "terrorism." Yet Trump allowed Erdogan to send in troops to push the Kurds out of much of Rojava.

Although the least discussed, Sudan experienced a most notable

---

13. See "Featuring Janan Aljabiri (Iraq), Rima Majed (Lebanon), and Gilbert Achcar (SOAS, University of London)." Accessible here: https://www.soas.ac.uk/ development/events/devstudseminars/21jan2020-special-panel-event-the-second-arab-spring-seasons-of-revolution.html

revolt with the overthrow Omar al-Bashir, in power since 1989. Bashir is now in prison, some of the most egregious forms of state oppression of women in the name of religion have stopped, and negotiations are underway with the Darfuris and other oppressed African minorities. Given its location at the southern borders of the Arab world, Sudan's revolt also resonated with unrest outside the Arab world, especially with the ferment in neighboring Ethiopia, underway for several years. Since the Bashir regime combined authoritarian Islamism with nationalist military rule, both military nationalism and Islamism emerged totally discredited, unlike in Egypt after 2011. A space for the left may have opened up. But at the same time, the new civilian leaders, who enjoy considerable popular support, have in no way crossed beyond the horizons of neoliberal capitalism, let alone capitalism itself. This is the agenda of a self-limiting revolution, one that stops at the political sphere. Positive change in the conditions of life and labor will occur only with the development of a radical class politics independent of the current civilian leadership, let alone the holdovers from Bashir who still control a major part of the state.

We have also witnessed social ferment in Europe, especially in France. A massive and persistent strike wave halted transport and many other state functions for nearly two months in December and January. Hundreds of thousands shut down their workplaces and joined street demonstrations week after week in the face of the neoliberal Macron government's proposal to cut pensions. France has one of the highest levels of life expectancy in the world, in large part because of the hard-fought struggles by working people after the 1944 liberation from Nazi occupation to make sure that many high-stress jobs allowed for earlier retirement without severe poverty, along with universal healthcare. The mass workers struggle of 2019-20 was preceded the year before by the militant Yellow Vests movement in more rural parts of the country, some of whose energies spilled into the recent strikes. 2019-20 has led in turn to the creation of militant leftwing networks not only among the youth, but also among transport workers. For now, the strike wave of 2019-20 has been defeated in the sense that the government may have outlasted them and has enacted its retrogressive new pension plan. Two possible reasons for this defeat stand out: One is that organized labor has not been able to tap into the vast reservoir of class and anti-racist anger that permeates the African and Arab communities in the big urban areas. A second is that French labor was left to struggle alone, with no other Europeans joining in with mass labor struggles of their own. However, in Ireland, a different sort of opening occurred in February, when the left-of-center Sinn Fein Party came out about even with the two big conservative parties, a breakthrough based upon anger over housing and medical costs.

The case of India is especially significant, because the Modi government has moved in an openly fascist direction and the resistance movement has been so massive and succeeded in breaking down some religious and caste divisions among the oppressed classes. In the past year, Modi removed all autonomy from Kashmir and placed it under lockdown; enacted an immigration law that excludes Muslims, who are 14% of the population; and developed a draconian law that would remove tens of millions from the citizenship rolls, mostly Muslims and members of the poorest and most oppressed parts of the working classes. At the same time, the resistance of Indian women, workers, students and intellectuals, and elements of the Muslim community has reached proportions not seen in decades. One of the most important actions was the occupation since December 16 of a major road in New Delhi's Shaheen Bagh neighborhood by women from the local Muslim community, who have received support from many sectors of the population. Significantly, they were joined by the young Dalit leader Chandrashekhar Azad, who underlined, "This is not only a political agitation" but one that gets to the core of what India will be as a country. Elderly Muslim women stood for weeks in the cold at the frontlines of the Shaheen Bagh occupation, with one of them declaring: "Let the police come, let them use their lathis [long batons], we will not budge until we have obtained justice."[14]

As our Indian comrades wrote recently, in the face of harsh

---

14. Quoted in *Le Monde*, January 19, 2020.

repression against the protesters, "it is Muslim women who are at the forefront of the protests. They have not only shown extraordinary courage to come out of their houses challenging the extremely patriarchal society to which they belong, but have also shown enough maturity to continue their protest tenaciously as well as peacefully in spite of several provocations. As a consequence, they have succeeded in gaining support from different quarters of society besides students. One shining example is opening of Langars (free kitchens) for the protesting women by poor Sikh peasants from around Delhi... The unique feature of these protests lies in the fact that they are neither led by any political party nor by any charismatic leader but by the collective leadership of the women and students. Similar protests are being held at several other places of Delhi along with the protests at Calcutta, Lucknow, Patna, Gaya, Bhopal, Raipur, Nagpur, Allahabad, Bombay, Jaipur, Chennai and countless other cities as well as villages."[15] Modi's total ban on all public gatherings and transport at the end of March is surely seen by him as a way to put an end to all that, but anger at the government's complete mismanagement of the coronavirus, which it initially ignored for months, may lead to a different result.

Meanwhile, the global environmental movement is surely not going away. Although it includes tendencies from anti-humanists who advocate drastically reducing the number of people on the planet to those who argue for a green capitalism, a deepening radicalization within it is evident. For example, on her recent trip to the U.S., 17-year old climate activist Greta Thunberg and her friends spoke with Native American activists at the Standing Rock Sioux reservation in North and South Dakota to get inspiration for how a society without emissions could be organized. In the talk delivered to the UN Climate Summit in New York, just after her trip to Standing Rock, she said, "You have stolen my dreams and my childhood with your empty words.

---

15. Parivartan ki Disha "Citizenship Amendment act (CAA) and National Register for Citizens (NRC) are Violent Attacks Against the Working and Oppressed Masses of India" in *The International Marxist-Humanist*, February 23, 2020. Accessible here: https://imhojournal.org/articles/citizenship-amendment-act-caa-and-national-register-for-citizens-nrc-are-violent-attacks-against-the-working-and-oppressed-masses-of-india/

And yet I'm one of the lucky ones. People are suffering. People are dying; entire ecosystems are collapsing. We are in the beginning of a mass extinction and all you can talk about is money and fairy tales of eternal economic growth. How dare you!"

For many, the Trump presidency is not only evidence of a failed democracy but also a frightening indication that the evils we knew existed in the U.S. would intensify and become acceptable. This has led to an increase in hate crimes, misogyny, displays of white supremacy (as in the horrific scenes in Charlottesville), nationalist policies such as the hyper-persecution of the undocumented, Muslim travel bans, and the separation and caging of families seeking asylum at the U.S.-Mexico border.[16] The separation of migrant children from their parents and the conditions under which they were jailed is an especially disturbing display of inhumanity that stands out even amidst a sea of unconscionable acts of violence. It shows once more that some forms of inhumanity cannot be justified for any reason and bring people together to fight across class, gender, race, and other markers of difference.

A similar example is the growing indignation and resistance of women. The misogyny evidenced by Trump during his campaign led to the Women's March, which brought women across the country in the hundreds of thousands and was supported by women across the world. In addition, the #MeToo movement gained significant appeal, beginning with the drive to end college rapes, followed by the move to denounce sexual assault and harassment in the workplace and the conviction of powerful, high-profile rapists such as Harvey Weinstein. Yet an important concern that continues to haunt these women's movements is the lack of attention and incorporation of these issues as they affect women of color.[17] For example, the contradictions that sometimes come between the interests of white

16. Monzó, Lilia D. & McLaren, Peter "Red love: Toward racial, economic and social justice" in *Truthout*, December 18, 2017. Accessible here: http://www.truth-out.org/opinion/item/28072-red-love-toward-racial-economic-and-social-justice

17. Oluo, Ijeoma "Women of Color Assess the Impact of The Women's March" in *Here & Now*, March 24, 2017. Accessible here: https://www.wbur.org/hereandnow/2017/01/24/women-of-color-march

women and women of color were evidenced in the Women's March. Originally organized by Black women, it was subsequently taken up and popularized by white women who proceeded to seek assistance and support of the police to maintain safety and "order." For women of color these images remind us of the very different ways in which the police interact with us.[18] Similar problems persisted in the #MeToo movement, which was initially organized by Tarana Burke, a Black woman, seeking to develop a project of healing for Women of Color. With little initial attention to this foundation, #MeToo was appropriated by predominantly white professional women and public figures. While there is no doubt that women publicly "coming out" to curtail the power of men who use their status, money, and positions to intimidate, harass, and assault women is not only commendable but necessary to challenge existing patriarchal relations, this does not change the fact that it was done without initial acknowledgment of Burke. Nor did they do enough to seek out the voices and insights – or *Reason*—of women of color or working-class women.

V

Although a complete breakdown of the global economic and political order cannot be ruled out today, that does not mean a new society will arise to take its place. The truly critical question is this: Once the COVID-19 pandemic recedes, will the social distancing, breakdown in face-to-face communication, and increased atomization that define the current reality become the new norm that defines the future? Or will movements arise that put an end to the abstract and indirect character of human relations under capitalism? For a positive outcome to take place, the system has to be *brought down*, through a conscious *movement* of masses of people. Socialism is the first form of society that arises from the conscious, purposeful activity of living

---

18. Chen, Tanya "People Have Strong Feelings About Cops High-Fiving People in the Women's March in Atlanta" in *BuzzFeed News*, January 23, 2017. Accessible here: https://www.buzzfeednews.com/article/tanyachen/cops-highfived-womens-marchers

subjects of revolution. It is not brought into existence by some blind force operating behind people's backs.

The *objective*, material condition for socialism remains the inherent non-viability of capitalism; the *subjective*, material condition for socialism is the struggles of masses of people against racism, sexism, class domination, and environmental destruction—of which many new manifestations are bound to emerge. But there is also an *immaterial* condition for socialism—the availability of a cogent conception of what life can be like without the domination of capital. *Ideas matter*; there can be no forward movement to freedom without them. And ideas are as immanent in the historical process as any material factor, as we can see by the unexpected resurgence of interest in socialism in the capitalist-imperialist heartland, the U.S. This provides a vital foundation for Marxist-Humanists to engage in today's discussions of socialism, as part of the effort to develop a viable alternative to capitalism that transcends the dead-ends of the past. To this end, we are working to publish a new edition of Marx's *Critique of the Gotha Program*.

In doing so, it is vital to pay heed to Marx's notion that "the transcendence of self- alienation follows the course of self-alienation." It is impossible to get to the absolute like a shot out of a pistol. Subjects of revolution first come to consciousness by battling the most immediate forms of oppression facing them. One of the most important of these is today's glaring social inequalities, which explains why the default option for most radical theoreticians remains advocating one or another form of "fairly" redistributing value. This should not be simply dismissed out of hand, since there is a need for a thoroughgoing redistribution of wealth. At issue is whether it can be achieved and sustained so long as we remain prisoners of a system based on augmenting value, or wealth in monetary form, as an end in itself.

As Martin Hägglund puts it in *This Life: Secular Faith and Spiritual Freedom*, "It does not make much sense to argue that the problem is capitalism and at the same time argue that the solution is the redistribution of capital wealth. Yet this argument is routinely made on the Left today. The form of the argument is a contradiction in terms: it asserts that the problem is capitalism and that the solution is capitalism. The contradictory form of the argument is covered over by a sleight of hand, whereby capitalism is tacitly defined as neoliberalism and redistribution is tacitly defined as an alternative to capitalism… Redistributive reforms can certainly be a helpful *means* for political change under capitalism. But even in order to understand the substantial challenges that our redistributive reforms will encounter…we need to grasp the contradictions that are inherent in the capitalist production of wealth."[19]

Such a perspective is not utopian, since many in today's movements oppose all sorts of economic inequality without stopping there, since they aim to recover a sense of humanity from the rebellion, the appropriation of spaces in their communities. New organizational forms have arisen that create community and shared responsibility in the face of an increasingly atomized and alienated world. In doing so, they are reaching to reconnect with the essence of what it means to be human—the capacity for conscious, purposeful, *collectively driven* activity.

For decades an assortment of theorists of the postmodern mode have held that separation and loss of unity is to be celebrated. *Différance* was upheld in opposition to abstract universals imposed by racist, sexist, and homophobic attitudes and structures. But lost sight of in this was the notion of a shared human project, without which any of our other projects, be they around class, race, or gender, ultimately fail to realize their potential. Marx referred to this as a "positive humanism"; Frantz Fanon called it a "new humanism." The quest for a *new* humanism continues to show itself today, even if many remain under the ideological thrall of the celebration of difference over universality. We must distinguish the abstract, *oppressive* universals that *claim* to be emancipatory (such as liberalism) from the *concrete universalism* expressive of what Marx called our *species-being*. To be sure, many claims to "universality" continue to exclude those who do not fit the default model of a white, male-dominated world. But we can hardly challenge the increasingly fragmented

---

19. Hägglund, Martin (2020). *This Life: Secular Faith and Spiritual Freedom*, New York: Pantheon, p. 383.

and alienated character of modern life by assuming away the need to recapture the *communal*. Only then can what Marx called "the realm of free individuality" arise. Our tasks center on articulating and developing a conception of new human relations opposed to the false universals of capitalism–racism–patriarchy. This is just as important as theorizing the transcendence of the capitalist law of value; in fact, one depends upon the other.

Chapter 2

The Seeds of Revolution Have Sprouted: What is Now to be Done?

By Peter Hudis

Based on report to a Convention of the International Marxist-Humanist Organization; discusses how the new turning point reached with movement for Black lives can deepen the development of a viable alternative to capitalism.

Part I: The Challenge of a New Historical Turning Point

Turning points in history are very rare. We are now living in the midst of one, with the two months of virtually continuous protests against police abuse, the criminal injustice system, and for a *human* society that have swept the U.S. as well other parts of the world since the police murder of George Floyd on May 25.

These massive and ongoing protests are defined by the clash between two absolute opposites—the forces of *death* embodied in police murder, racism, misogyny, environmental destruction, and the domination of dead labor (or capital) over living labor—and the forces of *life*, embodied in those aspiring for *human* emancipation.

Nothing displays the *deadly* part of that contradiction more than the decision of the Trump administration (supported by the *entire* Republican and much of the Democratic Party) to send hundreds of federal troops from the Department of Homeland Security and Immigration and Customs Enforcement to a dozen cities at the end of July to tear gas, beat, and arrest—often without warning or provocation—hundreds of protestors. This is not just a passing move aimed at bolstering Trump's support among the racist far-Right. It represents an effort to repress through direct *military* measures a movement that has so far proven uncontainable. Such repressive moves are bound to only intensify following the November election—especially if Trump refuses to acknowledge its results and leave office should he lose.

Exactly how this movement (which no one anticipated prior to its emergence at the end of May) will develop and progress we cannot yet know. But this we do know: when history suddenly surges forward, it isn't enough to just repeat what you said, did, or thought even weeks earlier. You either catch the historic current and move along with it, or you are swept backward relative to the new turning point that has been reached.

Turning points in history are exciting but also painful and difficult to live through. We need to be sensitive to this, as we try to *understand* what is going on.

The wave of protests that has occurred over the past two months is unprecedented. Multiracial events largely led by African Americans have occurred in 2,000 U.S. cities, towns, and rural areas. It is estimated that 26 *million* participated in protests in the U.S. alone. Most amazing, it has become an *international* movement. Protests against police abuse, racism, and social inequality have broken out in four dozen European and Latin American countries as well several in Africa and Asia, involving tens of thousands at a time. *This has never happened before.*

Chileans who were injured (and in some cases blinded) by tear gas and rubber bullets in protests there last fall are advising U.S. activists on how to protect themselves; anti-Assad activists in Idlib Province in Syria, the last remaining bastion of the opposition, have created an anti-racist mural in solidarity with the movement for Black lives. Dozens of such examples abound in other countries. As a friend in India wrote, "Could anyone even imagine what a worldwide wildfire a single spark in the U.S. has lighted up within so short a time? It is as if thousands of Arab Springs are happening simultaneously all over the world."

The protests are largely spontaneous—but not disorganized. On May 31, a Chicago artist who hasn't been active in left politics asked on his Facebook page if anyone was interested in holding a rally on the North Side; 24 hours later 5,000 showed up and marched for six hours. Countless other examples abound of such self-organization born from spontaneity. At the same time, grassroots activists who have long been part of the struggle to defund police and abolish the prison system have developed an array of new venues across the U.S. in the weeks after the first burst of protests at the end of May and beginning of June. It has brought together Native Americans, Asian immigrants, Blacks, Latinx, and white youth on a level not seen in decades.

Most important of all, the movement has reshaped political discourse in the U.S. Proposals routinely dismissed by liberals and tired radicals just months ago—defunding police, abolishing prisons, and reparations—are becoming mainstream. A large majority of the Minneapolis City Council has come out in favor of dismantling its police department. There are also calls to eliminate police unions, the most egregious protector of murderous cops. Recognition is growing that cops are not workers; they are instead *gendarmes of capital* who must be disarmed.

A lot has changed since we authored the document "Where to Begin? Growing Seeds of Liberation in a World Torn Asunder" in mid-April.[1] In recounting a series of important mass uprisings around the world in 2019, it noted, "No such mass revolts have occurred recently in the U.S." But we did add, "the same seeds of radical self-organized liberation" have been planted here. *These have now sprouted*, as seen not just in the size but the *form* of protests. These often differ from traditional marches in that they serve as vehicles for providing aid to impoverished communities and a forum for discussing issues and ideas. Women speaking out against sexual violence; immigrants opposing deportation; former prisoners decrying the lack of measures to prevent the spread of Covid-19; transgender people demanding their rights—all this and more are

---

1. See Anderson, Kevin B.; Hudis, Peter; Johansson, Jens; Ludenhoff, Karel & Monzó, Lilia D. "Where to Begin? Growing Seeds of Liberation in a World Torn Asunder" in *The International Marxist-Humanist*, April 10, 2020. Accessible here: https://imhojournal.org/articles/where-to-begin-growing-seeds-of-liberation-in-a-world-torn-asunder

given space to be heard. *Mutual aid* is one of the striking features of the protests, with assistance being provided in the form of food, water, medical attention and legal services at almost every event. What we cited from activists in the citizen assemblies of Chile in 2019 applies just as well to the situation many have experienced in these protests: "We are living a total break with the everyday life to which we were subjected. That's why the atmosphere is very special, invigorating and even joyful. We are recovering a sense of humanity from the rebellion, the appropriation of spaces in our communities."[2]

Clearly, this marks the most powerful threat to Trump since his election. But it is not just a challenge to Trump. Minneapolis is one of the most progressive cities in the U.S.; Clinton got 65% of its vote in 2016. Yet since 2012 only 1% of complaints against police abuse has led to disciplinary action. New York's Bill de Blasio, a liberal elected to end the "stop and frisk" policy against Blacks and Latinx, now defends police riots against protesters. And Laurie Lightfoot, Chicago's first Black woman Mayor, was one of the first to impose a curfew leading to hundreds of beatings and arrests—while supporting Trump's sending Federal goon-squads to Chicago after initially expressing opposition to it. Today's protesters are not looking to restore America to what it was before Trump, but oppose the whole edifice of neoliberalism that made him possible.

How could such a movement arise so fast, so unexpectedly? *A big reason is the pandemic*, which exposed racial, class, and gender inequities as never before. Big business getting massive bailouts while millions of laid-off workers got little or nothing; the net wealth U.S. billionaires increasing 15% during the pandemic while millions go hungry; Amazon and other companies ratcheting up production while not providing protective gear to workers—*the coronavirus class divide* is all too evident. So is the gender divide, as women forced to work from home face the double burden of caring for children off from school and ill relatives while receiving no compensation and little recognition. The racial divide is the most obvious of all, with Blacks suffering death rates twice that of whites and Latinx

---

2. Quoted in Juan Manuel Boccacci, "Citizen Assemblies Are Challenging the Neoliberal Model in Chile," *Orinoco Tribune*, Feb. 3, 2020.

workers (especially in meatpacking and agriculture) suffering from extremely high infection rates.

Since racism is the Achilles heel of U.S. society, and class relations have been structured along racial lines since its inception, revolts against racist dehumanization have historically served as the catalyst for challenging its dominant social relations. *And so it is today.* The protests have not detracted from the class struggle, they have enhanced it, by bringing into view the *deadly* ramifications of life under capitalism. Which is why so many from diverse backgrounds have joined it, *including working class whites.*

To be sure, the growth of new labor organizing during the pandemic helped prepare the ground for this. Strikes by bus drivers in Detroit, Amazon workers in Staten Island, meatpackers in Iowa and South Dakota, as well as labor protests in Brazil, Ivory Coast, Pakistan, Palestine, Kenya, Italy and Germany against the failure to protect workers' safety during the pandemic, all indicated (as Ron Herrera of the Los Angeles County of Labor put it a week before the murder of George Floyd), "we've been moving toward a worker rebellion."[3] But it took the response to his murder to bring all this to the surface, in a new, unexpected form.

In a word, we may now be witnessing a new kind of *multiracial working-class movement.*

After Biden won the South Carolina primary with significant support from African Americans, some questioned the relevance of the Marxist-Humanist concept of "Black Masses as Vanguard," developed over a 50-year engagement with U.S. Black freedom struggles. But they overlooked the importance of *youth.* Most Black youth either didn't vote in the primaries or went for Sanders. (He won the support of Black and Latinx voters under 35 in virtually every primary that he contested). And there is no question this new movement is led and driven by youth.

The generational gap within Black America has not gone away, any more than its internal class divisions. The two often go hand-in-hand, as seen in the number of Black corporate Democrats who

---

3. See Goldberg, Michelle "The Phony Class War" in *The New York Times*, May 19, 2020.

(along with Biden) are opposing the growing calls to defund police departments. A new stage of revolt does not only bring people together, it also accentuates the divide between those aiming to uproot the system versus those who want to maintain their place within it.

The central role of youth in the protests underlines the Marxist-Humanist conception, articulated by Raya Dunayevskaya as far back as 1958, that "Even though the youth are not directly involved in production, they are the ones whose idealism in the finest sense of the word combines with opposition to existing adult society in so unique a way that it literally brings them alongside the workers as builders of the new society."[4] White youth at rallies are holding up signs like "White Silence is White Compliance" and interspersing themselves between the police and the crowd so that people of color have less chance of being the first to be beaten by their batons. It is as if years of discussion and debate on race theory and white privilege has been absorbed by a new generation. The impact of this is likely to be felt far into the future, even as the movement experiences (as all do) ebbs and flows.

Precisely for this reason, the forces of bourgeois society are moving to attack the movement, discredit it, or coopt it into "safe" channels. This initially took the form of trying to impose a separation between "good, peaceful" demonstrators and "bad, violent" ones. It goes without saying that there are always adventurists who use protests for their own purposes, just vas there are bound to be agent provocateurs and undercover police out to create mayhem. But undifferentiated attacks on the looting and rioting that characterized early phases of the response to Floyd's death—as if violence against people is the same as against property—completely misses the point: namely, that the violence inflicted by racialized capitalism calls such actions into existence.

What Vicky Osterweil wrote about the Ferguson protests of 2014 speaks aptly to today: "In making a strong division between Good Protesters and Bad Rioters, or between ethical non-violence

---

4. *Constitution of News and Letters Committees* (1958), p. 2. The organization that still bears that name long ago failed to live up to such principles—which was a major reason for the formation of the International Marxist-Humanist Organization.

practitioners and supposedly violent looters—the narrative of the criminalization of Black youth is reproduced... Looting is extremely dangerous to the rich (and most white people) because it reveals, with an immediacy that has to be moralized away, that the idea of private property is just that: an idea, a tenuous and contingent structure of consent, backed up by the lethal force of the state. When rioters take territory and loot, they are revealing precisely how, in a space without cops, property relations can be destroyed and things can be had for free."[5]

Once it became clear that the vast majority of the protests were in fact peaceful, the effort to discredit them gave way to the claim (made especially by liberals) that posing such "radical" demands as abolishing police and prisons risks antagonizing potential "allies" and makes it easier for Trump to stir up "whitelash" against the movement. But as has become clear to anyone paying attention, Trump and his allies will paint anyone who takes action against state repression and police violence as a "dangerous radical"—he even accuses Biden of being one, who has long been an accomplice in augmenting the power of the police and criminal injustice system.

The fundamental divide opened up by the recent events is between two concepts of freedom. One side defines freedom as the atomized individual being free from all external constraints—especially those provided by the lives of other people. This is exemplified in Trump supporters protesting social distancing—with guns in hand. As one woman who refused to put on a face mask put it, "we have individual rights, we don't have community rights."[6] The other side defines freedom as the ability to actualize our human potential—central to which is care and concern for the lives of other people. This is exemplified in protesters insisting that the lives of others, especially *Black* lives, *matter*. These two irreconcilable definitions of freedom are based on radically different notions of the individual. One counterposes the individual to society, expressed by Margaret Thatcher as "society does not exist, only individuals do"; the other

---

5. Osterweil, Vicky "In Defense of Looting" in *New Inquiry*, August 21, 2014.

6. McFarquhar, Neil "Workers in Stores, Already at Risk, Confront Violence When Enforcing Mask Rules" in *The New York Times*, May 16, 2020.

expressed by Karl Marx as "the individual is the social entity"[7] and "society does not consist of individuals, but expresses the sum of interrelations within which these individuals stand."[8]

But make no mistake: this is no mere clash between two abstract, metaphysical notions of "freedom." It is a clash of ideas embodied in two antagonistic social forces. One is armed and backed up by the most powerful military on earth, the other is not.

As Frantz Fanon put it, "The natives' challenge to the colonial world is not a rational confrontation of points of view. It is not a treatise on the universal, but the untidy affirmation of an original idea propounded as an absolute. The colonial world is a Manichean world."[9]

The unanswered question is which concept of freedom will prevail. Answering this will depend on a fight to the finish, which has only just begun. All those who aspire for freedom and liberation need to become a party to the fight and not a mere bystander to it. And that fight involves a battle of *ideas*, which are never epiphenomenal or of secondary importance. Which idea of freedom will prevail—the one which seeks egoistic self-aggrandizement as an end in itself (which is the substance of capitalism), or the one that expresses humanity's ontological characteristic as social, *caring* beings (which is the substance of socialism)?

It is by no means assured that *consciousness* of the idea of freedom immanent in today's protests will lead to developing a viable alternative to capitalism. *Ideas* arise spontaneously from mass struggles, but a *philosophy* that can address *what happens after the revolution* does not. As Dunayevskaya put it, the consciousness that arises spontaneously from below "does *not* exhaust the question of cognition, of Marx's philosophy of revolution."[10] *If*, however, it is held that the social consciousness that arises from below *does* exhaust

---

7. "Private Property and Communism" in Marx, Karl & Engels, Friedrich (1975). *Marx-Engels Collected Works*, Vol. 3, New York: International Publishers, p. 299.

8. Marx, Karl (1973). *Grundrisse* (translated by Martin Nicholas), New York: Penguin, p. 265.

9. Fanon, Frantz (1973). *The Wretched of the Earth*, New York: Grove Press, p. 41.

10. Dunayevskaya, Raya (1981). *Rosa Luxemburg, Women's Liberation, and Marx's Philosophy of Revolution*, New Jersey: Humanities Press, p. 60.

cognition, it follows that a philosophy of revolution that can give spontaneous revolts a direction is completely superfluous. This is the approach that has been followed by many on the Left, which has resulted in an abdication of responsibility for providing a vision of the future that can point us beyond capitalism.

As Marx once put it, "We do not confront today's realities in a doctrinaire way with a new principle: Here is the truth, kneel down before it! We develop new principles for the world out of the world's own principles. We do not say to the world: Cease your struggles, they are foolish; we will give you the true slogan of struggle. We merely show the world what it is really fighting for, and consciousness is something that it has to acquire, even if it does not want to."[11]

Such consciousness is needed because once attained, the day of revolution cannot be far off. Here too we take our cue from Marx: "The recognition of the products as its own, and the judgment that its separation from the conditions of its realization is improper—forcibly imposed—is an enormous advance in consciousness, itself the product of the mode of production resting on capital, and as much the knell to its doom as, with the slave's consciousness that he *cannot be the property of another*, with his consciousness of himself as a *person*, the existence of slavery becomes a merely artificial, vegetative existence, and ceases to be able to prevail as the basis of production."[12]

Part II: Can Anti-Racist Movements Help Elicit an Alternative to Capitalism?

The people see the punishment, but it does not see the crime, and because it sees punishment where there is no crime, it will see no crime where there is punishment.

—Karl Marx, "Debates on Thefts of Wood"

Given today's events, we can expect a further growth of interest in socialism—indeed, it has been happening since the Great Recession

---

11. "Letter to Arnold Ruge (September 1843)" in Marx, Karl & Engels, Friedrich (1975). *Marx-Engels Collected Works*, Vol. 3, New York: International Publishers, p. 144

12. Marx, Karl (1973). *Grundrisse* (Martin Nicholas's translation), New York: Penguin, p. 463.

of 2008. The combined impact of the Covid-19 pandemic and the response to police killings has so highlighted the bankruptcy of capitalism that the quest for a socialist alternative is bound to reach new levels.

However, we have a problem: Socialism is largely understood today as the "fair" redistribution of surplus value and profit. This is to be expected, given today's unparalleled levels of social and economic inequality. However, while calls for redistributing wealth can be helpful in mobilizing opposition to capitalism, they are inherently self-defeating since they leave untouched the social, class, and human relations that define the capitalist mode of production and reproduction. Redistributing surplus value assumes the continued existence of value production—a system based on augmenting wealth in monetary form as an end in itself. After all, one cannot redistribute what does not exist. Such a standpoint defines the new society by the principles of the old one. It is impossible to develop a viable alternative to capitalism on this basis.

To obtain perspective on this problem, let's turn to history. Massive socialist movements emerged at the end of the nineteenth century, and a number of them came to power in the twentieth century. Virtually all of them defined capitalism as an anarchic market economy based on private property, and socialism as a planned economy based on nationalized or socialized property. This was quite understandable, since prior to the 1930s capitalism was a highly anarchic, unplanned, and competitive system.

But what happened when a new *global* stage of capitalism emerged in the 1930s—*state-capitalism*? It took the form of Stalinism in the USSR, Nazism in Germany, and FDR's New Deal in the U.S. We know what happened when it came to Stalinism: those who defined the new society as a planned economy based on nationalized property embraced so-called "socialism" in the USSR (and later Mao's China) even as democracy was negated in favor of a totalitarian single party state. Not all who supported such regimes were bad people: some were serious revolutionaries. But they suffered from a narrow understanding of capitalism and socialism which led them astray. However, we also have to pay attention to what happened to the "democratic socialists" who also believed that socialism is defined by social planning and socialized property. They too capitulated to the new stage of state-capitalism by endorsing FDR's New Deal and the Keynesian welfare state whose aim was to save capitalism. By no accident, many of these Social Democrats also ended up supporting U.S. imperialism.

By the end of the twentieth century, when the bottom fell out from the Keynesian welfare state and "Soviet-type" societies, virtually all of them— democratic socialists and Stalinists alike—had capitulated to existing capitalist society. So extensive was this that the "death of Marxism" was proclaimed around the world (often by its former adherents).

What does this tell us? A defective understanding of capitalism and socialism becomes *deadly*, especially when a turning point is reached with the rise of a new stage of capitalism.

But what about the movements of the 1960s? They too were massive and spontaneous, and many in them embraced socialism by the 1970s. But did a conception of socialism arise that broke with the narrow Social Democratic and Marxist-Leninist idea that socialism equals nationalized property? Sadly, it did not. One part of the New Left gravitated back to Social Democracy, while another took the plunge into one or another form of "Marxist-Leninism" centered on building "a vanguard party to lead." No fundamental rethinking of the meaning of socialism emerged from either one. That was true of even the most revolutionary dimensions of the 1960s. Few were more revolutionary than the Black Panthers, whose militancy and revolutionary propagation of mutual aid inspired an entire generation; yet while they initially embraced a series of independent radical perspectives, most of its members ended up embracing Maoism—just in time for Mao to betray the Black struggle by rolling out the red carpet for Nixon.

Unlike the 1930s, which gave us state-capitalism, or even the 1970s, when it slightly mutated into what many call neoliberalism, today we are not facing a new stage of capitalism. We are instead facing the *decay* of capitalism, which can no longer fulfil its mission of revolutionizing the means of production and providing a better life for masses of people. A decaying economic system spews forth a decaying political superstructure, personified in such despicable characters as Trump, Bolsonaro, Duterte, Netanyahu, Orban, Erdogan, and Putin. All they have to offer is egotistical self-aggrandizement run amok.

These personifications of capital (Trump included) have however done us a big favor: they allow everyone to finally see what capitalism is really made of. There is no going back to the "third way" of the Blairs and Clintons who painted our exploitation in pretty colors. The only way is to move forward, by developing a new concept of socialism that is adequate for our life and times.

But there is no assurance we will get there, since today most people continue to define socialism as the redistribution of value—which is based on the old notion that capitalism is defined by market anarchy, and socialism by social planning. So, what we can we do to move the discussion of a genuine alternative to capitalism forward?

I wish to pursue this by exploring whether the anti-racist struggles and movement for Black lives provide a basis for reconceptualizing socialism beyond the limits of redistribution.

We have heard it said many times in the past weeks that people of color have been excluded from the social contract. But what does this *mean*? In capitalism wage labor takes the *form of appearance* of a contract. Workers agree to sell their labor power to capitalists, who agree to pay them a wage. *Mutual recognition* takes place insofar as each agrees to acknowledge (at least formally) the claims of the other. But recognition on the level of wage labor is limited and superficial, since the capitalists extend recognition to the workers only insofar as they provide them with surplus value, while the workers extend recognition to the capitalists only insofar as they continue to employ them. Recognition is therefore purely *juridical*—but it does take place.

But what happens when race enters the picture? To make a contract with someone, you have to acknowledge, at least on some level, that they are a person. But what happens when whites "see" Blacks not as persons but as *things*? This is of course the essence of racism. When the person is Black there is no recognition even on the juridical level. Their personhood, their *humanity*, is not seen at all. This is what makes it so easy for racist police to kill with abandon.

Since humanity is comprised of *social* beings, and society is a *product* of the social contract, those outside the contract are viewed as not truly human. As Frantz Fanon argued, the very *being* of Blacks becomes problematic in a racialized society. This barrier to formal, juridical recognition is very painful. But there is a positive in this negative. Since victims of racism have weaker ties to juridical relations, their revolt has the potential to go beyond calls for a "fairer" distribution of the products of labor by questioning the *dehumanized* character of social life itself.

In a psychiatric paper that has recently become available, Fanon notes that since Blacks are excluded from the social contract they often refrain from cooperating with the police and other authorities. Cooperation depends on a contractual relation—which is absent for people of color. He writes, when "I confess as a citizen I validate the social contract."[13] But if society does not view you as a person you have no stake in the contract: "There can be no reintegration if there has been no integration."[14] Hence, anti-racist revolts challenge the very basis of existing society.

However, it is always possible to reduce the struggle for recognition to a plea for acceptance by the forces of *existing* society. Such pursuits are fruitless, since capitalism acknowledges people only insofar as they are embodiments of economic categories—insofar as they are viewed as things...which is the very basis of racism to begin with! We need a revolution precisely because our humanity cannot and will not be recognized in capitalism. But what kind of revolution? *And what kind of socialism?*

Surely not one that treats race and gender as secondary to class. All workers have ethnic, racial and gendered attributes. Advocates of a "class first" position tend to abstract from all this. Ironically, this is exactly how "the worker" appears from the standpoint of capital: as a mere bearer of labor power, the expenditure of undifferentiated labor in the abstract. Viewing people abstracted from the life-world of their lived experience may be adequate from the standpoint of capital, but it is completely inadequate for those trying to become

---

13. "Conducts of Confession in North Africa (I)" in Fanon, Frantz (2018). *Alienation and Freedom*, London: Bloomsbury, p. 415.

14. Ibid, p. 412.

free from capital's dominance.

Likewise, a "revolution" limited either to a social-democratic program of income redistribution or a centralized state plan fails to address the real aim of the class struggle—the abolition of abstract or alienated labor, which to Marx, is the *substance* of value. In contrast, as Fanon put in in another paper, "Labor must be recovered as the humanization of man. Man, when he throws himself into work, fecundates nature, but he fecundates himself also."[15]

In sum, uprooting capitalism *as well as racial and gendered oppression* can only be achieved by multiple forces of liberation that seek not mere juridical acknowledgment of their suffering but a *revolutionary* transformation of the very fabric of human relations. I believe the objective conditions for achieving this are being generated today by the logic of capital.

Capitalism is internally driven to augment value by reducing the relative proportion of living labor to dead labor at the point of production. Relatively fewer workers become employed in productive labor (or labor that produces surplus value), while the number of unemployed and underemployed grows. However, the working class as a whole actually *increases* in size as fewer are employed at the point of production, since expanded reproduction depends not just on the *production* of surplus value on also its *realization*. A host of new occupations open up to ensure the latter (information technology, service work, etc.). Contrary to the claims made by some, the working class is larger today than ever before—over 3.5 billion people. A worker is defined as someone who does not own the means of production and does not play a supervisory role for those who do. However, because of the extremely high organic composition of capital that defines contemporary capitalism, today's concentration and centralization of capital tends to produce not a compact and unified working class but rather a highly differentiated and variegated one employed in multiple arenas.

As living labor becomes detached from the direct process of production and becomes more precarious, workers' connection to the

---

15. "The Meeting Between Society and Psychiatry" in Fanon, Frantz (2018). *Alienation and Freedom*, London: Bloomsbury, p. 530.

contractual form of appearance of wage labor becomes increasingly tenuous. Workers entering the labor market today can expect to change jobs half a dozen times during their lives. As a result of their more precarious existence, workers tend to no longer obtain even the pretense of recognition from the personifications of capital, since they are increasingly displaced from having a direct connection to them. The struggle for recognition seems to hit a dead end...and yet every human being does want to be recognized. So, what then?

As capitalism deprives recognition to those who once received it on a *minimal* level, some become moved to identify with those to whom recognition has always been denied on any level. Battles over of race, gender, and sexuality increasingly serve as the catalyst for bringing a differentiated and dispersed working class onto the streets. We may be witnessing something like this today, with the possible emergence of a multiracial working-class movement.

The Covid-19 pandemic reminds us that life is fragile, precious, and short. It is above all *finite*. We have no choice but to manage as well as we can our finite time. Let's engage in pursuits, projects, and debates that develop an alternative to capitalism. That choice is one of *life versus death*.

Chapter 3

COVID-19 and Resistance in Brazil: Life-Making, Memory, and Challenges in Seeding an Alternative Future

By Rhaysa Ruas

Report presented to the July 2020 Interim Convention of the International Marxist-Humanist Organization.

When COVID-19 – a pandemic caused by a pathogen that sprouted from the very conditions through which our capitalist societies produce food and deal with nature – was announced as a reality in Rio de Janeiro on March 13th, our concerns were focused on growing police killings, lack of water in various working-class neighborhoods, and an increasing unemployment rate at a national level of 12.2% (around 12.9 millions of people),[1] this in a labor market where informal work comprises as much as 41% of all workers[2] and where many of the unemployed are therefore not counted. Austerity politics were on track, putting forward a project of deeper privatization, financialization, income concentration, and social exclusion. State

---

1. This is the national official data, that does not count those who have stopped looking for a job, for example. Specialists say that, with this additional group, numbers can easily be estimated as 24.3%, i.e., 27.7 million people. See more at: Alvarenga, Darlan; Silveira, Daniel. "Desemprego sobe para 12,2% no 1º trimestre e atinge 12,9 milhões" in Portal G1, April 30, 2020. Accessible here: https://g1.globo.com/economia/noticia/2020/04/30/desemprego-sobe-para-122percent-em-marco-e-atinge-129-milhoes.ghtml

2. Quintino, Larissa. "Informalidade atinge 41% dos brasileiros, maior taxa em 4 anos", in Veja, January 31, 2020. Accessible here: https://veja.abril.com.br/economia/informalidade-atinge-41-dos-brasileiros-maior-taxa-em-4-anos/

budgets for social expenses such as health and education have been frozen until 2036, according to a constitutional amendment approved in 2016.[3] An escalating political crisis that involved all levels of state power was also part of this atmosphere.

Very quickly, the political crisis – at the center of which was the battle between President Jair Bolsonaro and the Congress and the Supreme Court – turned also into an internal fight between the President and his own ministers, including the former Minister of Health[4]. Whilst the latter was inclined to follow World Health Organization (WHO) directives, Bolsonaro insisted on denying the full existence of the virus while also calling public demonstrations against democracy. As I am writing this report, Brazil reached more than 50 thousand COVID deaths – second highest in the world – and, after several splits in the government, Bolsonaro has not even nominated ministers for education, culture, or health.

Although the corporate mass media has been positioning itself on the side of "science," highlighting a degree of concern for public health, unequal social realities have been more naturalized than really addressed. The media showed three main general concerns regarding virus contamination. First, came the virus's quick pace as it spreads in favelas and peripheries, where it is far from uncommon for a whole family to share a one-room house, with a lack of sanitation, clean water and other infrastructure. Importantly, when the federal government offered an emergency aid of USD 112.96 per month for the poor – after proposing the ridiculous amount of USD 37.65 per month ending with a political battle with the left in Congress – it was 8 times less than the

---

3. The ceiling amendment, also known as "the amendment of the end of the world," freezes state budgets for social policies for 20 years and was approved right after the institutional coup that led to the impeachment of former President Dilma Rousseff. For more, see Alessi, Gil. "Entenda o que é a PEC 241 (ou 55) e como ela pode afetar sua vida", in *El país*, December, 13, 2016. Acessible here: https://brasil.elpais.com/brasil/2016/10/10/politica/1476125574_221053.html

4. Lee, Bruno; Schiavon, Fabiana; Queirolo, Gustavo. "Relembre quatro meses de episódios explosivos da crise política em meio à pandemia", in *Folha de São Paulo*, December, 31, 2020. Accessible here: https://www1.folha.uol.com.br/poder/2020/03/relembre-episodios-explosivos-da-crise-politica-em-meio-ao-coronavirus.shtml

necessary salary calculated for the basic market basket, USD 868.94. This process also revealed the further extension of the reality of social marginalization, since many of those requesting the benefit faced real challenges in requesting it, such as no internet access or required documentation (basic citizen ID), not to mention the unreasonable delays in payments – issues which were once more naturalized.

The second concern was Brazil's prison system, containing the third biggest population in the world. Here, the scenario of general human rights violations and lack of infrastructure would create a dramatic effect that *could go outside its walls*. Importantly, the general concern on the part of the dominant media was not with human beings stuck there to die (even if 41,5% of them have no criminal convictions[5]), but the fear that COVID could spread outside its walls, for which the measures taken – prohibition of family visits[6] and no policy for guaranteeing their health or well-being – are illustrative.

A third concern, less noticed and even less addressed, was Indigenous and Quilombola people's vulnerability to contamination, including the more isolated communities that were already suffering constant invasions and attacks increasingly legitimized by the Bolsonaro administration. Again, much more was said than done, since no state policy was directed at them and the virus got there through the same roads opened by the invaders. Those invasions are part of a bigger complex scenario of conflicts and disputes over land, such as the looting of Amazon forest – another project driven by Bolsonaro.[7]

Although mainstream media, NGOs, and civil society – mostly

---

5. Barbiéri, Luiz Felipe. "CNJ registra pelo menos 812 mil presos no país; 41,5% não têm condenação", in Portal G1, July, 07, 2019. Accessible here: https://g1.globo.com/politica/noticia/2019/07/17/cnj-registra-pelo-menos-812-mil-presos-no-pais-415percent-nao-tem-condenacao.ghtml

6. Family visits are pretty much the only source of better food, soap/hygiene items and support incarcerated people have. The prohibition has a huge impact over this population lives and living conditions.

7. In another piece, I addressed the contours of this project, which also lies in an acceleration of capital context. See Ruas, Rhaysa "The Amazon Burns and the Politics of Death: Resisting the Commodification of our Future" in *The International Marxist-Humanist*, August 31, 2019. Accessible here: https://imhojournal.org/articles/the-amazon-burns-and-the-politics-of-death-resisting-the-commodification-of-our-future/

rooted in the liberal-oriented, progressive middle classes – showed a degree of preoccupation with the so-called social question, far less was said when the first COVID death in Rio de Janeiro was a domestic worker, a Black woman residing in a peripheral area, who was infected after being forced to work in her employers' house even after they had returned from Italy with symptoms. Considered to be essential workers and with few or no labor rights, domestic workers, such as maids, nannies and housekeepers kept working in precarious situations with no support and very little concern for them or their families' health.

II. Building survival strategies in trenches...

When a Black man named George Floyd was brutally murdered in the U.S. by the Minneapolis Police Department on May 25th, we had already counted 23.522 COVID deaths in Brazil and at least 606 police murders[8] in Rio de Janeiro State alone, of which 78% victims were Black[9]. What is shocking is that even after a severe social isolation decree, police brutality against Black people continued to increase: In April 2020, there were 43% more such killings than at the same time last year[10]. Meanwhile, during the months of April and May 2020, the state of Rio de Janeiro increased the volume of police operations, allegedly meant to crack down on drug trafficking, by 27.9%. This produced 53% more deaths than in the same period of the previous year[11]. Floyd's murder vocalized again a slogan that

---

8. Official data collected until April 2020, accessed on May 26, 2020. For more or current numbers, see: ISP. Dados Abertos do Instituto de Segurança Pública do Rio de Janeiro. Accessible here: https://www.ispdados.rj.gov.br:4432/

9. Rodrigues, Matheus; Coelho, Henrique. "Pretos e pardos são 78% dos mortos em ações policiais no RJ em 2019: 'É o negro que sofre essa insegurança', diz mãe de Ágatha", in Portal G1, June 6, 2020. Accessible here: https://g1.globo.com/rj/rio-de-janeiro/noticia/2020/06/06/pretos-e-pardos-sao-78percent-dos-mortos-em-acoes-policiais-no-rj-em-2019-e-o-negro-que-sofre-essa-inseguranca-diz-mae-de-agatha.ghtml

10. Ibid.

11. Ibid.

shows the worldwide working-class's most recurrent feeling: WE CAN'T BREATHE. We cannot breathe because capitalism as a system is unbreathable. In regulating our access to the means of subsistence, thereby forging the specific kind of precarious, disciplined life that is necessary to maintain capital's drive for profit, capitalism is a death-making system. What can we do when a system like that is revealed for the whole society? How not to let this historical opportunity opened by US popular revolt and the appearance of COVID-19 – a neoliberal pandemic – vanish into a re-naturalization of capitalist barbarism, i.e. "going back to normal"? More concretely, how to live and make a living in a world like that? At the current juncture, all our political work seems to be limited to harm-reduction actions, but it is our duty as Marxists to make sense of those contradictions and push them forward.

For instance, just as U.S. antiracist demonstrations have a core anti-capitalist and antiimperialist potentiality – since they stand against a state that brings inside its territory the same kind of military occupation that is carried out by its troops abroad, with curfews, police brutality and so on – they also have double imperialist impacts on countries like Brazil[12]. U.S. imperialism manifests itself in both violent and not always explicit forms, with a very marked cultural component that involves posing as a symbol of democracy and freedom while exporting militarization and forms of punitive discipline through its transnational industrial-military-prison complex. At this juncture, Brazilian white elites felt compelled to adopt an antiracist language and position – with our biggest TV broadcasters inviting Black journalists to speak on their main news

---

12. By saying the antiracist demonstrations have an imperialist impact in dependent capitalist countries, I am not blaming them – or any popular resistance/organization – for this. On the contrary, here I am just pointing to a structural dimension of a contradictory social form that, "built on the backs" of the U.S. working-class, and, more importantly, looking forward to open a debate with the U.S. radical left on the challenges of transnational resistance that account for the effects of imperialism. I argue that the very fact that U.S. imperialism historically also exports forms of resistance and cultural behavior, gives the U.S. left a bigger responsibility in terms of conceptualizing their own forms of resistance in a global perspective.

programs – progressive sectors were divided between (1) those grasping the moment in less radical terms, from a rights/equality language perspective and wanting to reproduce U.S. political struggles and demonstrations in terms of expanding the politics of inclusion and diversity, and (2) those who understood the revolts in their anticapitalist dimension and wanted to use the conjuncture to push forward a more radical project here in Brazil.

The current institutional left generally held the first position, and during the electoral calendar for municipalities and senates, maintained an agenda of trying to advance Blacks, women, and LGBTQI+ people in power positions. This is the platform adopted by the left parties represented in Congress, with the support of progressive NGOs. Guiding its politics by the electoral contest with no real alternative project for transcending current social relations, the bigger socialist party (PSOL) called timidly for industrial reconversion, while focusing – equally timidly – on a call for Bolsonaro's parliamentary impeachment. They left out any call for the taxation of big fortunes, for example.

In the second, more radical position, we can find grassroots collectives and social movements from favelas and peripheral areas – mostly Black and Indigenous. But within a political and economic context like the one described above, they are also the ones who are carrying the burden of guaranteeing working class survival, especially in favelas, villages and peripheries. This sector, composed of several collectives, spontaneous mutual aid networks/actions, community-based organizations, and supported by few non-electoral/revolutionary socialist parties or anarchist organizations, are comrades who are planting the seeds for a possible alternative future. They do so at a high personal cost for their activists and their own organizing. Nevertheless, since the very beginning of social isolation, it is the Black favelas' youth, organized in collectives, that are in the frontline of the fight against the virus and its social effects. They work to guarantee not only the basic means of subsistence to the majority of poor families, but also information about the virus and how to prevent it. Many were spontaneous mutual aid initiatives, although this sector also comprised important collectives that have been confronting state violence in the frontline of antiracist struggles of the past years.

In my view, we can classify the urban working-class mobilization during the pandemic, i.e., resistance through solidarity for survival, into two big groups: actions of political pedagogy (education, advocacy and mobilization) and actions aimed at guaranteeing the reproduction of life (life-making actions). In the first group, we can locate 1) the dissemination of information and fighting against widespread government fake news, 2) the work of popular communicators in informing people how to act in case of COVID-19 deaths and domestic violence, 3) collecting frontline workers reports and then helping to denounce and protest over issues like the lack of PPE's, 4) institutional advocacy work regarding state's accountability and to stop police violence, 5) mothers and parents of state violence victims demanding state accountability, 6) human rights protections and immediate liberation of imprisoned people, also putting forward a prison abolition movement, 7) online political organizing and education, with online classes and debates; and finally 8) organizing public street demonstrations.

In the second sector we can locate actions like 1) getting individual and institutional donations in order to distribute food, clean water, hygiene kits, etc., 2) giving health and funeral support in favelas, villages and peripheries, where those state services do not reach, 3) guaranteeing survival in prisons and detention centers, including within the socio-educative system. The collectives also organized to sanitize the streets in favelas, since the state refuses to do so to the full extent that is needed in those communities. They also responded to the fact that most people in those areas had difficulties maintaining social isolation (recall that those are the neighborhoods where many of the essential workers live, e.g., cleaners and janitors, domestic workers, care givers, food makers, and transportation services).

What can all those movements – and Brazilian reality – bring us in terms of conceptualizing/thinking revolution/social transformation? If/how does it connect to the US uprisings?

Brazilian mutual aid actions maintain in their daily praxis a long tradition of popular solidarity and dual power in areas where the state historically has been present only through military/punitive force. Since colonial times, Blacks, Indigenous people and the working poor have created and lived in autonomous territories. While they were more and more subsumed by capital, even today we have areas where the state does not penetrate very much, and self-organization is a general form. Key examples include many Indigenous and Quilombola communities and Black communitarian organizing, especially in favelas whose history often confuses itself with urban Quilombos (although in favelas, as organized crime more and more keeps close relations with the state, this has become rarer over the years). This has happened either by communities' resistance and the possibility of keeping isolated or through the lack of a state presence as a social insecurity mediator in those communities. Right now, for example, there are self-organized Indigenous self-defense groups, such as Guardiões da Floresta (Forest Guardians), that are defending their territories in regions such as the Amazon from looting and deforestation by direct confrontation with invaders, as well as illegal hunters, lodges, gold miners, and so on.

In general, Latin America has a lot of autonomist experiences, most notably the Zapatista movement, which furnishes us with lessons about how to keep police and the state out of daily life-making. Many of those autonomist experiences recover, maintain and/or preserve Indigenous, African and Specific Latin American cosmogonies, which bring to the movements' center another relationship between human beings and nature, and of the particular and the universal, where life-making is not driven by profit-making. Also present in some of those experiences is the understanding that police or state control is not only an objective institution, but also a relationship, an historical and ongoing process.

I would also like to call attention to the fact that the kind of debates raised worldwide after George Floyd's murder and the popular revolts that exploded in the US were already being addressed on a daily basis here, from defunding and abolishing the police to abolishing prisons and fighting against anti-Black genocide, to dual power experiences. Those kinds of debates are already an urgent issue, a key demand, and a part of a long-lasting reflection in the whole of Latin America.

Riots with cars and buildings burning after a killing committed by the police are a recurrent reality for activists from Rio and São Paulo favelas, although almost never broadcast in the mass media, which is completely controlled by corporate or state interests. Nor are such issues supported by the middle classes. But while the U.S. uprisings show the limits of a Black politics of inclusion and diversity, pointing in a more radicalized, anti-capitalist direction, Brazil's left strategy tends still to reinforce an old politics limited to inclusion/diversity. Can Brazil's grassroots and spontaneous mutual aid movements not only point this out, but also put forward an alternative direction?

It is not by coincidence that while the LA police department – one of the most lethal ones in the US – killed 601 people in the last 7 years[13], with just one criminal conviction, Rio de Janeiro police killed 606 people from last January to May 2020, with no convictions at all.[14] Here, I do not bring Brazilian particularity to this debate in order to do an Othering, or simply to measure it quantitatively as worse or better than US reality. I bring it up because paying attention to the particularity of Brazil's dependent capitalism helps us understand better the deeply racialized and gendered logic of global capitalism without reifying the US imperial character and role within it.

As I mentioned earlier, police brutality and a genocidal public security policy made "staying at home" even more impossible for most residents of favelas, with constant shootings and police operations. On May 20, an 18-year-old Black man was killed during a food distribution action at Cidade de Deus. The group was stuck in the middle of the shooting and recorded everything. Jota Marques, a comrade from *Frente Cidade de Deus*, told a local newspaper that when they questioned the police who did not want to let them go during the shooting, a policeman shouted, "If they didn't want to be shot down, they should not leave their homes

13. Kitonga, Ndindi "Black Lives Matter Uprising in Los Angeles: Working Toward a New Humanist Society" in *The International Marxist-Humanist*, June 13, 2020. Accessible here: https://imhojournal.org/articles/black-lives-matter-uprising-in-los-angeles-working-toward-a-new-humanist-society/

14. Ibid.

without having a Bible on their hands".[15]

Finally, on May 31 after the brutal murder of two more Black teenagers in Rio – inside their own houses – we had our first public demonstration: "Black and Favelas' Lives Matter: stop killing us". This demonstration was organized from the night into the day, when those favela activists decided that it was impossible to continue in the way they had been. The call for the demonstration stated: "We went to the streets because they came to kill us at home." The demonstration took place in front of the governor's palace, and although it was very peaceful and lasted only 1 hour – a decision of the movements that organized it in order to diminish COVID propagation and avoid confrontations with the police – the police still reacted with brutality, leaving one injured and another arrested. One week later, on June 7, we had another, bigger and more organized demonstration, this time in Rio's downtown. This time the police were more organized. With horses and military tanks in the streets and with a ratio of 2-3 police per demonstrator, they tried to curtail the protest, threatening civilians with their display of force and military power, arresting 40 people for no legal reason (with the excuse that they had sanitizer in their possession), forbidding the use of megaphones, making unauthorized personal searches, and encircling the protest. With the mass media covering the whole demonstration and its taking place in broad daylight, no real confrontation happened, but the police nonetheless sent a message of intimidation.

Even more concerning was the reaction of civil society to those brave and significant demonstrations. Many leftist intellectuals and activists, NGO members, artists, and digital influencers urged collectives in favelas to step back from organizing demonstrations. Their pressures included social media posts against the demonstrations. Their main argument was the possibility of those demonstrations giving Bolsonaro the excuse he needed to finally proceed with the expected military coup and formally close Congress

---

15. Aidar, Bruna. "Grupo que distribuía cestas básicas em comunidade fica preso em tiroteio", in Metrópoles, May, 20, 2020. Accessible here: https://www. metropoles.com/brasil/policia-br/grupo-que-distribuia-cestas-basicas-em-comunidade-fica-preso-em-tiroteio

and the Supreme Court. Others pointed to the fear that if we had more radical protests like in the U.S., we could have had a civil war, since this would give Bolsonaro reasons to fully liberate the right to carry guns in an already polarized civil society. Finally, a considerable part of the older generation of the Black movement warned that demonstrations could increase the spread of COVID in a scenario where we already have crowded hospitals and have not yet reached the peak of the pandemic, which would increase mortality within an already fragmented Black community. All those positions revealed an incorrect understanding of the workings of political formations and the meaning of power, since they grasp political power neither as a concentrated phenomenon nor as a social relation in an ongoing, historical process. Instead, they treat power as diffuse and "the coup" as an event in search of a cause. This is further evidence for the needed retheorization of capitalism and a work of rescuing radical concepts and the diffusion of revolutionary theory within Brazilian society.

III. ...but trying to think beyond capitalism: what alternative?

How to think about policing as a social relation? In a similar vein, how to put forward a call for defunding the police and reinvesting in social welfare, in a dependent capitalist and deeply militarized country? Is it possible to apply the same calls for defunding the police and reinvesting in social programs to dependent capitalist states like Brazil, considering the ways imperialist countries export their social problems and feed their welfare systems with Global South resources, blood, and sweat? What about US imperialism and the global system of militarization? More concretely, how can we abolish the police without creating a situation where private militias and death squads – already a part of Brazilian history as the origin of the police institution itself and now as parallel organizations with deep connections with this same institution, and with the state and dominant classes in general – could proliferate, undermining even more possibilities for civil society to control and denounce abuses, thus aggravating Black and Indigenous genocide? Finally, how to understand anti-Black genocide both in Brazil and the U.S.? Do they have similar meanings and processes?

In Brazil, as in other dependent economies, the super-exploitation of labor – the lengthening and intensification of the working day and the payment of wages below the normal value of the labor-power necessary for worker's subsistence and reproduction – is systemic. This raises several questions about the character of Brazil's citizenship model and to what extent racial structural inequalities cannot be diminished. Households, communities, and favelas serve as the main site that compensate for the lack of income necessary to guarantee daily subsistence. These communities thus become crucial sites of struggle for living standards and of resistance against capitalist exploitation. As a result, they also become the target of state violence. Gender and race relations thus help produce the devaluation of certain social groups and guarantee the reproduction of exploitation and expropriation.

In this scenario, one of the most pressing needs for retheorization in light of the experience of Rio's more radical social movements seems to be the relationship between anti-Black violence and capitalism (the capitalist quest for value). An understanding of capitalism as social totality can also help us avoid a reading of racism and anti-Black genocide that reproduces a dualistic framework, according to which it happens because Black people are completely disposable for capitalism, since we constitute "surplus" labor power. Predominant in contemporary literature, these readings are not only wrong, but mystify the very workings of capitalist society, by using a functionalist explanation – Black people's so-called disposability under capitalist system – to explain anti-Black genocide. Against this, I argue: we are killed precisely because we are indispensable for this system's functioning, and it is by producing differences in the access to means of subsistence and conditions of exploitation that capitalism produces the forms of life necessary for its own sociality. As I see it here, following social reproduction theorists[16], there is a contradictory relationship

---

16. Bhattacharya, Tithi. "How Not to Skip Class: Social Reproduction of Labor and the Global Working Class" in (Ed.) Bhattacharya, Tithi (2017). *Social Reproduction Theory: Remapping Class, Recentering Oppression*, London: Pluto Press, pp.68-93. See also Ferguson, Susan (2020). *Women and Work: Feminism, Labour, and Social Reproduction*. London: Pluto Press.

of dependency between the capitalist system and life's production processes and institutions: the existence of capitalism depends as much on the production of a healthy and fit global working class as on the maximum exhaustion of the individual worker within a particular nation state. In the course of the process of an inherently expansionary accumulation of capital, the capitalist class seeks to stabilize the reproduction of the labor force at a low cost and with a minimum of reproductive labor. This means, concretely, the reproduction of human life in destructive conditions, so that capitalism builds the life it needs; it replaces bodily life, incarnated, with an alienated form of social life, through a process of abstraction such as that presented in the transformation of concrete labor into abstract labor.[17] In this process, historically constituted along gendered and racialized lines, the level of access to resources for the reproduction of life determines the fate of the working class as a whole, also determining the specific forms of resistance of the different fractions that compose it. Now, although there is a tendency towards the total subsumption of human labor under capital, against this continuous tendency of compression and destruction of the means of production of life, the working class, "as a unified or fragmented force in sectors in competition, strives to conquer the best possible conditions for its renewal,"[18] and thus subsumption is never total.[19]

In this sense, all capitalist societies produce and reproduce constantly their own "Negro" and that is why we cannot combat genocide with inclusion and diversity politics, as it generates nothing but the reorganization of a social hierarchy that will produce its own new "Negro" in the future. How to think about this in Brazil, where Black people are more than a half of the total population? Here, a

---

17. This argument appeared for the first time in Ruas, Rhaysa "A crise da Covid-19 e o desvelamento das dinâmicas de produção da vida no capitalismo: um comentário à Tithi Bhattacharya" in (Ed.) Gonçalves, Guilherme Leite (2020). *Covid-19, Capitalismo e Crise: bibliografia comentada*, Rio de Janeiro: LEICC e Revista Direito e Práxis, pp. 180-190.

18. Vogel, Lise (2013). *Marxism and the Oppression of Women: Toward a Unitary Theory*, Chicago: Haymarket Books, p. 163.

19. See also Ferguson, Susan (2020). *Women and Work: Feminism, Labour, and Social Reproduction*. London: Pluto Press.

discussion about dependent capitalism and the specifically Brazilian social formation can be very important and illustrative, but this is rarely carried out.

I am not excluding the importance of the politics of inclusion, and even less am I suggesting that we return to a dualist debate, reviving old polemics around recognition vs. redistribution. For me it is clear that recognition is an integral part of class struggles/politics. What I am saying is that when we allow inclusion to become our only focus, guided by an idealistic U.S. civil rights model and without grasping the specific workings of capitalist social forms such as the State or Law, this politics turns quickly into its opposite. We cannot expect to combat a centuries-old ongoing genocide by idealizing a social or welfare state that never existed fully even in imperialist countries. Thus, the only way we can support, even critically, the fight for inclusion is as a tactic. But in posing the politics of inclusion and diversity as a tactical objective, we must protect and support the most radical movements within it. Making concessions, whether morally or discursively (against looting for example) is not only to help send our brothers and sisters to death but it also buries the concrete possibility of a better future for all. Such concessions are guided by a wrong interpretation of the State and the Law: as if we could change their own structural logic by just changing chess pieces. This ignores how the structures themselves are (only relatively) autonomous under capitalism to the extent they are reproduced "on the individual's backs." By crystalizing historical social praxis, incorporating them into the state's own ideological and bureaucratic structures, these structures can easily limit even the most radical political leader or demand by individuals or groups, turning them into their opposite while adapting them to their own logic.

The systemic challenges being faced, and the multiple forms of resistance (and survival) through solidarity found within the Brazilian working class during the COVID-19 pandemic, point toward the need for a retheorization not only of a broader antifascist and antiracist struggle, but also to the theorization of a real alternative to capitalism. The present seeds of unity between antifascist and antiracist struggles in Brazil have the potential to move us toward a deeper understanding of capitalism that can radicalize current democratic struggles. To be sure, we should keep to a formal democratic openness contra Bolsonaro, for it is fundamental to determining future modes/capacity of working-class organization. But our organizing to maintain democracy cannot be done in idealistic or narrow terms. It is not by chance that it is difficult to get the masses to support democracy when most of them have never really lived or experienced it. It's most difficult to convince people of the need to restore funding to the state when the state means only violence and corruption to many. But is this the only possibility for resistance, or there are others that can push us forward in the direction of a real social change?

As Peter Hudis[20] points out, capitalism has already shown that all it "can offer the future of humanity are social and natural conditions that are bound to become worse than those affecting us today." As a Black Marxist-feminist, I believe that if there is a future, it depends on the immediate social reorganization of life and production. As a Marxist-Humanist, I understand that this is only possible through the transcendence of alienation and of the form of value/social-property relations.

What can we do concretely *right now* towards the abolition of capitalism? I am arguing that in order to transcend alienation and the social division of labor, i.e., transcend value, what we actually need is a daily and permanent revolution. This can transpire only if we collectively raise our consciousness to the extent of being self-reflexive every second of our lives, in all of their aspects: moral, ethical, religious, questioning all our beliefs and the very way we treat people, all of this together. Given the totality of this system, how to be anti-racist? How to be anti-fascist? How to be anti-sexist? How to be anti-capitalist? Problematize everything, doubt, and question everything. Racialize and gender all discussions. Look for information. Hear and support those who are in the frontline of the struggles. Understand your history and your own experiences as integral to a broader class experience in its diversity, in light of

---

20. Hudis, Peter (2012). *Marx's Concept of the Alternative to Capitalism*, Chicago: Haymarket Books, p. 2.

a global capitalist system. But this cannot be merely a self-help program; it needs to be done at the level of political organization and be constitutive of multiple positionalities without losing sense of the totality they constitute in their diversity. The pandemic, the revelation of essential workers/life-making work and the solidarity chain it raises all across the world gives us a new condition of possibility in this direction.

How can we begin to move current resistance actions further? First: we need to archive our praxis and make sense of our collective radically-built knowledge. In other words, we need to make sense of our history in a collective way, not only in a formal academic sense, but also transcending it through the voices and experiences of the "uncertified", the mass of ordinary people whose stories and lives are uncounted (independent if they had access to formal education or not), as Choudry and Vally[21] put it. I am referring here to the radical and revolutionary political experiences of Black people, Indigenous people and the working poor in the Brazilian social formation, more specifically to the experiences of spontaneous and "uncertified" sectors of the working-class. This must be an intra-class project, a project that, by making sense of all standpoints within the working class – through the recognition of the social totality involving all social relations of oppression and exploitation in which their form of appearance seems to be autonomous – but with none as hegemonic, actually fights on a daily basis against attempts by the bourgeois standpoint make itself dominant, imposing already existing social forms. It cannot be intra-race, it cannot be intra-gender, but it must be intra-working-class, because although racism and sexism as forms of prejudice are deeply built into different fractions of the class, and thus of its consciousness, those oppressive relationships can be transcended only by concrete common struggle and political change over time.

On the other hand, racism and sexism as differential forms of exploitation and expropriation – i.e., oppression that impede sectors of the working class's access to their means of subsistence and

---

21. (Eds.) Choudry, Aziz & Vally, Salim (2018). *Reflections on Knowledge, Learning and Social Movements: History's Schools*, New York: Routledge, pp. 1-2.

production – are overdetermined by class differences that impede this common struggle itself. This is because, while the struggle ignores those deep class differences – concrete social-property relationships – the intra-race-only or intra-gender-only struggle necessarily move from common concerns to individual ones, just as property moved from common to individual, where capitalistic individual social-property relations tend to subsume the conditions of possibility of broader collective struggles for collective forms of social-property relations. The recent post-independence history of many African countries, for example, can illustrate how new Black and Indigenous dominant classes can be easily formed even when deeply political, anti-colonial struggles are taking place. Again, this is not to make a class-first claim but to recover the idea that classes exist only in concrete terms, i.e., in a racialized and gendered way and vice-versa, both in Brazilian or any other specific forms of capitalism.

By the year 2020, we, proletarians of the whole world, have had enough working-class organizing experiences within the State and the Law to collectively make sense of this process and to advance. And for the first time, we are so closely connected that we can easily archive those experiences in a transnational way. Thus, we have no need, given all the technological advances and transnational connections we already have, to still conceiving narrow national solutions to global problems or to be constantly repeating formulas that went wrong everywhere else in the 1960s, 1970s, 1980s, 1990s, because "maybe they would fit since our reality is different." On one hand, we need to find our own ways, by analyzing our own people and their challenges – which is, as Frantz Fanon tell us, a huge challenge to the colonized, because the first and very deep issue is to recognize ourselves: "Who am I?"[22] On the other, we need to connect and reflect those paths to a broad, transnational context, accounting for other specific paths to the same goal. Those questions can only be answered – and the solutions can only be found – by creating our future by facing the injustices of our global, common, past.

---

22. Fanon, Frantz (1973). *The Wretched of the Earth*, New York: Penguin.

Chapter 4

Battle of Ideas: Race, Class, Gender, and Revolution in Theory and in Practice

By Ndindi Kitonga

Report to the July 2020 Interim Convention of the International Marxist-Humanist Organization, slightly updated.

Introduction

Ours is the age that can meet the challenge of the times when we work out so new a relationship of theory to practice that the proof of the unity is in the Subject's own self-development. Philosophy and revolution will first then liberate the innate talents of men and women who will become whole. Whether or not we recognize that this is the task history has 'assigned', to our epoch, it is a task that remains to be done.

—Raya Dunayevskaya, *Philosophy & Revolution*

Over the past 10 years, we have seen the rise of authoritarianism, state repression and white supremacy across the globe. As always, Black, Indigenous people of color, youth, women, LGBTQ folks, and people with disabilities will often bear the brunt of these dehumanizing structures. Some of the structural issues Black and Brown populations are experiencing in the United States at this time, include over-policing, police brutality, gentrification of already under-resourced communities, depressed wages, lowered health outcomes, housing insecurity, mass incarceration to name a few.

Marxist-Humanism is a philosophy that engages with the totality of Marx's work, posits that alienation is at the center of dehumanizing structures humans face under capital and embraces Marx's philosophy of liberation. To analyze the current uprisings we must try to understand the dialectical relationship between the objective and subjective forces in these movements. This report will examine issues of race and gender from a United States based context. Because we are living through an unprecedented time, of a Black-led multi-racial movement, this report will primarily focus on United States-based Black and feminist movements.

The Movement of Black Masses

Racism, specifically, is the state-sanctioned or extralegal production and exploitation of group-differentiated vulnerability to premature death.

—Ruth Wilson Gilmore

BLACK LIVES MATTER AND RELATED MOVEMENTS

Each generation of revolutionaries must theorize, and act based on current conditions. Movements like Black Lives Matter have been at the forefront of not only fighting police violence, the incarceration of Black, Brown and Indigenous people, and an unjust immigration system, but have also taken on issues such as mental health, LGBTQ rights, and reproductive justice for folks of color. Moreover, the current Covid-19 pandemic has not revealed a "we're in this together" moment as many in the bourgeoisie were claiming it would. In fact, this particular crisis has laid bare all of the inequities in our society as Black, Indigenous People of Color (BIPOC) find themselves disproportionately affected by this catastrophe. Indeed, the social and economic impacts of this crisis coupled with recent racist murders of Black folks is fueling the revolts we see as BIPOC, women, youth, the working class, immigrants and sexual minorities rise up against the domination of racialized and gendered capitalism.

Throughout this decade, the United States public has been forcefully confronted with what many communities of color have long understood, i.e. their bodies are considered disposable in this society. A 2015 study by the Harvard Public Health Review confirms this, revealing that Black men are three times more likely to have a fatal encounter with the police compared to white men. The same study also shows there's been a sharp rise in these fatal incidents since the 1980s.[1] The 2014 brutal murders of Eric Garner and Michael Brown by police mobilized the Black masses to say, "I can't breathe," a reference to Garner's last words as police manhandled him cutting off his circulation and "We have nothing to lose but our chains," a phrase found in the *Communist Manifesto* but popularized by Assata Shakur in the 1970s. Today we repeat the same harrowing last words of George Floyd as he pleaded for his life and called out for his mother, while a police officer kneeled on his neck for 8 minutes and 46 seconds. "I can't breathe" is now the cry of the streets as masses everywhere protest Mr. Floyd's murder, racialized capitalism and state violence worldwide.

Public perception of the movement for Black lives and of systemic racism have shifted over the past 7 years. A July 2020 poll by Langer Research Associates reveals that 63% of U.S. Americans support the Black Lives Matter movement and 69% of the same group acknowledge that Black people and other racialized minorities face institutional racism within the criminal justice system[2]. The response to the question of systemic racism has jumped 15 percentage points since 2014, the year the Black Lives Matter movement was born. This shift in consciousness for the masses does not necessarily translate into widespread desire for revolutionary change. At a time when confidence in law enforcement institutions is at a 30 year low (48% across the general population, 56% among whites and 19% among Blacks), the U.S. masses favor widespread police reforms over defunding or abolishing the police.[3] White U.S. citizens are less likely to support the

---

1. Krieger, Nancy et. al. "Trends in US deaths due to legal intervention among black and white men, age 15-34 years, by county income level: 1960-2010" in *Harvard Public Health Review*, Vol. 3, January, 2015. Accessible here: http://harvardpublichealthreview.org/190/

2. Langer Research Associates "63 Percent Support Black Lives Matter as Recognition of Discrimination Jumps" in *Langer Research*, July 21, 2020. Accessible here: https://www.langerresearch.com/wp-content/uploads/1214a3RaceandRights.pdf

3. Brenan, Megan "Amid Pandemic, Confidence in Key U.S. Institutions Surges" in *Gallup*, August 12, 2020. Accessible here: https://news.gallup.com/poll/317135/amid-pandemic-confidence-key-institutions-surges.aspx

defunding of the police department budgets and shifting resources to social programs (41% compared to 49% of the Hispanic and 70% of the Black population). And while the U.S. general population does not support the complete abolishment of policing as we know it (15% support from the general population BUT 33% for persons under 35 years old), the public is now having important conversations about the carceral state.[4]

Keeanga-Yamahtta Taylor carefully examines the superficial display of solidarity we are witnessing from our public and private institutions. "At one level, the rapid, reflexive default to offering symbolic recognition of racism was quite typical. No other country engages in the cavernous nothingness of the fake apology as frequently as the United States."[5] At the same time she acknowledges what other radical scholars have that the uprisings are a response to prolonged systemic inequities minorities suffer under racialized capital and that the emerging social movements are forcing everyone, including the left to engage seriously with issues around class, race, anti-blackness, crime, and state-sanctioned violence.

An important task for those in these movements is to offer a critical analysis of the role of looting and vandalism during protests. As Vicky Osterweil and others have noted, the media attempts to distinguish "good" protesters from "bad" ones and by doing so "reproduces racist and white supremacist ideologies, deeming some unworthy of our solidarity and protection, marking them, subtly, as legitimate targets of police violence. These days, the police, whose public-facing racism is much more manicured, if no less virulent, argue that 'outside agitators' engage in rioting and looting. Meanwhile, police will consistently praise 'non-violent' demonstrators, and claim that

---

4. Crabtree, Steve "Most Americans Say Policing Needs 'Major Changes'" in *Gallup*, July 22, 2020. Accessible here: https://news.gallup.com/poll/315962/americans-say-policing-needs-major-changes.aspx

5. Taylor, Keeanga-Yamahtta "We should still defund the police" in *The New Yorker*, August 14, 2020. Accessible here: https://www.newyorker.com/news/our-columnists/defund-the-police

they want to keep *those demonstrators* safe."[6] In this current revolt, the "good" protesters can be seen marching during the day, chanting and expressing anger in a way that is only slightly unacceptable in civil society. The "bad" protesters are characterized by actions like looting, ignoring curfews, vandalism, mocking police officers, allowing their anger to spill over onto freeways by occupying them, and displaying generally antisocial behavior. Embracing the "good vs. bad" protester logic risks dividing movements and undermining the solidarity protesters might otherwise have. This logic also implies that those engaged in these acts don't have agency and are not involved in conscious and tactical resistance. Furthermore, undermining the more violent aspects of a revolt underestimates the very visceral rage many are experiencing at this time. Organizers and activists should continuously push their demands forward and not fall into this logic, particularly at a time when we see the state making concessions and wide public condemnations of systemic racism. Conversations about non-community invaders should center on police and National Guard troops who are the true outside agitators as they've been deployed from other cities to repress communities. Moreover protesters can and have been using this moment to push forward a counter-narrative, using the language of looting, stealing and violence to confront the white supremacist settler-colonial project that is the United States, and making the case that exploitation under capitalism is actually the ultimate form of looting.

The current Black Lives Matter movement has been viewed as a form of race-based identity politics by some on the Marxist left who remain only interested in class-first solutions to the problems we experience under capitalism. These critics claim that these forms of identity politics undermine class solidarity for neoliberal reforms or for bourgeois individualisms. Understanding that the politics of recognition do not develop in a vacuum, Raya Dunayevskaya did not reject these politics wholesale, in fact she evokes Hegelian concepts in support saying, "it is clear that for the Black masses, Black

---

6. Osterweil, Vicky "In Defense of Looting" in *The New Inquiry*, August 21, 2014. Accessible here: https://thenewinquiry.com/in-defense-of-looting/

consciousness, awareness of themselves as African-Americans with their dual history and special pride, is a drive toward wholeness. Far from being a separation from the objective, it means an end to the separation between objective and subjective. Not even the most elitist Black has quite the same arrogant attitude as the White intellectual toward the worker, not to mention the prisoner."[7]

Dunayevskaya recognizes something that scholars like Taylor point to, that even the Black elites in the United States society cannot escape racialization.[8] This is an important observation that the class-reductionists are usually not able to make. Their fear of being derailed from struggling against a global class war prevents them from understanding how comparatively little power Black and Brown elites hold in a racist society. They also fail to realize that even the bourgeois Black and Brown classes are willing to fight against racialized oppression and have historically done so. Indeed, almost all United States mainstream politicians of color at our present time are willing to proclaim, "Black Lives Matter."

Concerning the issue of identity-first or race-based movements, Dunayevskaya also rejects the idea that Black self-development of subjectivity is bourgeois. Over the span of her career, she remains committed to the struggle against structural racism and its relationship to capital. She also follows the activities and self-development of people of color, particularly in relation to the Black dimension in the United States. Determined to always get to the root of racial domination, she was consistently willing to take the class-reductionist left as well as the Black bourgeois leadership to task. Dunayevskaya does more than champion the rights of racialized minorities or simply explain how their oppression is connected to a larger class war. Through her dialectical exploration of history, she is able to demonstrate that not only are the United States Black populations always on the forefront of liberation movements but that no system of domination can snuff out the human desire to be free.

---

7. Dunayevskaya, Raya (1982). *Rosa Luxemburg, Women's Liberation and Marx's Philosophy of Revolution*, Urbana: University of Illinois Press, p. 281.

8. Taylor, Keeanga-Yamahtta (2016). *From #BlackLivesMatter to Black Liberation*, Chicago: Haymarket.

In *American Civilization on Trial: Black Masses as Vanguard*, she writes, "[the Black dimension] at each turning point in history, anticipates the next stage of development of labor in its relationship with capital. Because of his dual oppression, it could not be otherwise."[9] To make this claim she analyzes the creativity of abolitionists through the slave revolts, Black anti-imperial resistances during the turn of the 20th century, Black labor battles of the reconstruction era, the courageous actions of the Little Rock Nine in their quest to desegregate schools and the Black wildcat Detroit strikes — notice that many of the struggles she highlights have no obvious or immediate class character. Dunayevskaya takes a special interest in the 1955 Montgomery Bus Boycott asserting that this struggle was as relevant and radical as the Hungarian revolution that occurred the year after. She writes extensively on not only the relatedness of these movements but on the underlying humanism that propels them. Throughout her scholarship, Dunayevskaya observes that the Black masses at this time remain revolutionary, "contrary to the reports in the white press, Black America's actual rejection of white capitalistic-imperialistic exploitation, with or without Black lackeys, is, all one and the same time, a time-bomb that is sure to explode, and a time for thinking and readying for action."[10]

BLACK PAIN FOR WHITE WITNESSES

In a provocative essay Zoe Samudzi explores the question of why we watch videos of Black people being murdered or brutalized by state actors or white vigilantes. She asserts, "it serves usually, as a reinscription of white supremacy: a reification of the boundary between the white self and the black 'others' through a passive bystander witnessing and the enforcement of race through public violence."[11] In other words, it

---

9. Dunayevskaya, Raya (1963). *American Civilization on Trial: Black Masses as Vanguard*. Chicago: News & Letters, p. 81.

10. Dunayevskaya, Raya "A Post-World War II View of Marx's Humanism, 1843-83; Marxist-Humanism, 1950s-1980s" in *News & Letters*, 1986, p. 12.

11. Samudzi, Zoe "White Witness and the Contemporary Lynching" in *The New Republic*, May 16, 2020. Accessible here: https://newrepublic.com/article/157734/white-witness-contemporary-lynching

is possible to view these heinous acts over and over again, express concern, and share the videos for the purpose of awareness-raising without actually engaging in anti-racist praxis. If state violence is a mainstay of Black life, what awareness is there to raise? Why have the masses at this point not come to understand how violence functions under racial capitalism?

Samudzi also claims that "the killings, in a way, become a macabre method of marking social and political time" and an opportunity for white progressives and leftists to claim moral superiority over other white people because they experience sympathy by watching the horror and subsequently sharing them in a quest for justice (that as we've seen is rarely achieved). One other reason for the sharing of these videos is to convince the masses of the innocence of the victims. If Black people in this society by default are guilty, then there must be evidence of the opposite before the masses can demand justice for their murders. The families of state murder victims understand this and also often urge us not to look away from the dehumanization of their Black family members. What remains clear is that we will continue to witness violence against Black, Brown, Indigenous, non-male, queer and disabled folks until we fundamentally change social relations in our societies. We will continue to share and be horrified by the videos that capture this violence. One question we should ask is how to move mass passive white viewership from this place of witnessing to one of struggling for justice. Perhaps we are on the way there as the witnessing of George Floyd's murder has become the impetus for the current uprising against state violence.

WOMEN'S MOVEMENTS AND ABOLITION FEMINISMS

Let this (moment) radicalize you rather than lead you to despair.

—Mariame Kaba

We've seen tremendous activism and organizing of women (many of color) and queer folks over the past several years. In 2019, we witnessed Sara Nelson, the head of the flight attendants union call for a general strike after a government shutdown left TSA screeners, air traffic controllers, and customs agents unpaid for 35 days. This tactic has not been attempted in the United States for over 70 years! Although flight attendants are paid by the private airlines they work for, Nelson made a rousing speech calling for worker solidarity across all sectors, "Some would say the answer is for them to walk off the job. I say, 'What are you willing to do?' Their destiny *is* tied up with our destiny — and they don't even have time to ask us for help. Don't wait for an invitation. Get engaged, join or plan a rally, get on a picket line, organize sit-ins at lawmakers' offices." Perhaps Nelson like many have recognized, the current political and economic conditions have opened the door for these radical ideas to be broached and the masses are hungry for changes. She would go on to say, "I think what we're seeing, with the teachers strikes, the hotel workers who took on Marriott and won, is that people are not willing to put up with it anymore. People are willing to do more to fight for their families because they have been pushed so far, and there has been so much productivity put on the backs of the American worker without any increases in wages." When asked about her call for a general strike, she wondered, "What is the labor movement waiting for?"[12]

While we have yet to observe a general strike, we cannot discount the strikes and other labor-related activities that have occurred over the past few years. Indeed, we've witnessed widespread teacher strikes in states like West Virginia, Oklahoma, Arizona, California and Colorado. These teacher strikes can be understood as both labor and feminist issues, considering that 77 % of all K-12 educators in the United States are female, and that the demands educators have been making address matters of social reproduction.[13] As teachers during these strikes have demanded better pay and/or work conditions, they've also called for changes that socialist feminists

---

12. Grabar, Henry "What Workers Can Learn From 'the Largest Lockout in U.S. History'" in *Slate*, January 25, 2019. Accessible here: https://slate.com/business/2019/01/sara-nelson-flight-attendant-union-strik-tsa-shutdown.html

13. Loewus, Liana "The Nation's Teaching Force Is Still Mostly White and Female" in *Education Week*, August 15, 2017. Accessible here: https://www.edweek.org/teaching-learning/the-nations-teaching-force-is-still-mostly-white-and-female/2017/08

everywhere have considered important for life-making. These include a demand to invest in counselors, librarians and mental health support for students, re-investment in after-school and early education programs for public education, access to quality education for working-class students, access to quality food in schools, and demands for the safety of children, and specifically, a halt to random searches and the policing of students.

One framework socialist feminists of color are rallying around particularly when it comes to issues of social reproduction, is that of abolitionist feminism.[14] Abolitionist feminism is an anti-capitalist framework with Marxist roots which seeks to not only dismantle the carceral state but project a new world. According to Maureen Mansfield, "abolitionist feminism invites us to consider the world we want, and how to organize to build it. Seeking a world beyond cages, policing and surveillance, Abolitionist Feminism focuses our attention on developing stronger communities and bringing about gender, race and economic justice. It encourages us to consider our approach systemically and collectively rather than individually... Abolitionist Feminism asks us to consider the violence and harm caused by the state, as well as inter-personally, and seek alternative strategies for addressing these harms."[15]

While abolitionist frameworks are not new, we find new generations of feminists of color adopting these ideas. The abolitionist frameworks are indeed informing activists and theorists in this moment of civil unrest. When the Black Lives Matter movement launched in 2014, most calls for justice from even the leaders of the organization were reformist in nature. In this second wave of BLM activism, we are witnessing these demands change to have a more abolitionist character. The present-day abolitionist movements comprise of grassroots organizers, feminist collectives and scholars and is a

14. Lober, Brooke "(re)Thinking Sex Positivity, Abolition Feminism, and the #MeToo Movement: Opportunity for a New Synthesis" in *Abolition: A Journal of Insurgent Politics*, January 2018.

15. Mansfield, Maureen "What is Abolitionist Feminism, and Why Does it Matter?" in *The Progressive Policy Think Tank*, June 13, 2018. Accessible here: https://www.ippr.org/juncture-item/what-is-abolitionist-feminism-and-why-does-it-matter

very decentralized movement. Beyond the abolitionist frameworks that unite their work, the organizing principles are carried out in context-specific ways. By eschewing big party politics, vanguardism or hierarchical organizations, abolitionists have managed to be nimble and propose an abolitionist platform that meets the current Black Lives Matter uprising. For example, the calls to #defundpolice and for #carenotcops were crafted quite thoughtfully. When abolitionists proposed these demands, they looked at actionable ways of approaching police abolition that had the potential to shrink the scope of policing, the size of the prison-industrial complex and to undermine the surveillance state. Defunding the police and investing public monies in services for communities that are most affected by the carceral system, creates the potential for new communities of care where societal ills are no longer addressed through either interpersonal or state violence.

By contrast, liberal reformers are calling for a police reform program known as #8cantwait.[16] This platform proposes measures to combat police brutality that many states have tried with little success (e.g. banning chokeholds on arrest victims) to ones that are almost unenforceable (e.g. mandating police officers to use de-escalation techniques in their arresting practices). These proposals seek to make tweaks to a system that can not be accountable to itself and offers no generative community-based to address peoples' material needs. But for the ongoing radical organizing of contemporary abolitionists, this framework would be accepted as the most progressive solution to the problems of state violence and police terror we face. So strong was the opposition to the #8cantwait program that its original framers have almost abandoned it and a collective of revolutionary abolitionists have released their own plan titled #8toabolition.[17]

Abolitionist frameworks have the potential of upending all systems of domination and projecting new humanist alternatives. As famed abolitionist feminist Mariame Kaba says, "a big part of the abolitionist project... is unleashing people's imaginations while

---

16. 8 Can't Wait Platform: https://8cantwait.org/
17. 8 to Abolition Platform: https://www.8toabolition.com/

getting concrete — so that we have to imagine while we build, always both."[18] Abolishing the carceral state would necessitate the abolishment of capitalism. The current abolitionist feminisms we are witnessing are advocating for a politic that goes beyond the redistribution of resources and instead proposes new human social relations that are not based on commodification and exploitation. This framework refuses to explore the "woman question," "the race question" or the "prison/policing/surveillance abolition question" after the revolution but demands that it be theoretically worked on now. Time will tell if these and related movements can potentially uproot the capitalist mode of production and overcome the mental and manual division of labor that creates alienated human relations.

Conclusion

Historically, pandemics have forced humans to break with the past and imagine their world anew. This one is no different. It is a portal, a gateway between one world and the next. We can choose to walk through it, dragging the carcasses of our prejudice and hatred, our avarice, our data banks and dead ideas, our dead rivers and smoky skies behind us. Or we can walk through lightly, with little luggage, ready to imagine another world. And ready to fight for it.

— Arundhati Roy

We therefore now need to initiate the exploration of the new reconceptualized form of knowledge that would be called for by Fanon's redefinition of being humanas that of skins (phylogeny/ontogeny) and masks (sociogeny). Therefore bios and mythoi. And notice! One major implication here: humanness is no longer a noun. Being human is a praxis.

— Sylvia Wynter

At the current moment, we are facing a global pandemic and multiple historic political uprisings. How are we to identify and be in solidarity

---

18. Duda, John "Towards the horizon of abolition: A conversation with Mariam" in *The Next System Project*. November 9, 2017. Accessible here: https://thenextsystem.org/learn/stories/towards-horizon-abolition-conversation-mariame-kaba

with the revolutionary subjects of our day? What kinds of organizations do we need at this time and what role can Marxist-Humanists play in articulating a theory of organization that meets this moment? It is abundantly clear that the masses are eschewing vanguardism and hierarchical organizations for smaller, more horizontal democratic female and queer-led models. As we theorize about organization, we should consider Dunayevskaya's insights when asked to address the question of decentralization within the Womens' liberation movement. She writes, "the demand for small informal groups is not to be disregarded as if it were a question of not understanding the difference between small and large, and that large is better. Nor can this demand be answered in our bureaucratic age by attributing to Women's liberation a deep-down belief in private property, petty home industry, and "of course" Mother Earth. Nothing of the kind. The demand for decentralization involves the two pivotal questions of the day; and, I might add, questions of tomorrow, because we are not going to have a successful revolution unless we do answer them. They are, first, the totality and the depth of the necessary uprooting of this exploitative, sexist, racist society. Second, the dual rhythm of revolution: not just the overthrow of the old, but the creation of the new: not just the reorganization of objective, material foundations but the release of subjective personal freedom, creativity, and talents. In a word, there must be such appreciation of the movement from below, from practice, that we can never again let theory and practice get separated. That is the cornerstone."[19]

Over the past two years we've explored matters of identity, intersectionality, and other politics of recognition in our theorizing around this issue. In the past I have suggested, "instead of becoming frustrated with the consciousness-raising and empowerment projects some identity-based movements have turned to, we should position ourselves to do the theoretical and practical labor required to be in critical solidarity with Black and Brown movements." I have also proposed that these projects be taken on by theorizing around the psychic components of racialized and gendered oppression while

---

19. Dunayevskaya, Raya (1982). *Rosa Luxemburg, Women's Liberation and Marx's Philosophy of Revolution*, Urbana: University of Illinois Press, p. 108.

seeking out ways to move incomplete articulations of intersectionality and emerging movements to a place of radical criticality. In addition, my fellow IMHO colleague Lilia Monzó asks us to move Dunayevskaya's concept of Black masses as vanguard to what she calls women of color as vanguard, making a case that women of color subjects are currently the *force and reason* for revolution.[20] Others in our organization like Peter Hudis propose developing an intersectional historical materialist framework that can theorize not only around Marxist concepts but also take on the issues of dehumanization produced by racialized and gendered domination under capitalism.[21] These are important additions to Marxist-Humanist thought as much of the revolutionary movement work we see today is being led by Black, Brown and Indigenous women and queer folks in the United States who are wrestling with similar questions.

Dunayevskaya always had a long and dialectical view of history and would systematically relate capital's latest crisis to mass movements and issues concerning people of color. She did so by developing Marxist-Humanism, a philosophy that reanimates the totality of Marx's Marxism and that posits alienation at the heart of the dehumanization we suffer under capital. She remained situated in the struggles of the day, paying special attention to the activities of the Black dimension which she identified as historically being an important force for liberatory movement. Always working from Marx's concept of revolution in permanence, she also posed the question "what comes next," taking care to articulate the potential to produce new humanisms during each revolutionary struggle. As the Marxist left continues to struggle when it comes to issues of race and gender and as identity-based intersectional theories continue to be relevant we are also noticing a liberatory politics emerge from below as people try to make sense of their everyday experiences. Our task as revolutionaries is to project better alternatives that take the everyday

---

20. Monzó, Lilia D. (2019). *A Revolutionary Subject: Pedagogy of Women of Color and Indigeneity*. New York: Peter Lang.

21. Hudis, Peter "How is an Intersectional Historical Materialism Possible? The Dialectic of Race and Class Reconsidered" paper presented at the Historical Materialism Conference, Toronto, April, 2019.

material conditions of folks seriously, to be in critical solidarity with the revolutionary subjects of our day and to "recognize that there is a movement from practice — from the actual struggles of the day — to theory; and, second, to work out the method whereby the movement *from theory* can meet it."[22]

***

Several excerpts of this report can be found in the chapter "Raya Dunayevskaya on Race, Resistance and Revolutionary Humanism" in *Raya Dunayevskaya's Intersectional Marxism: Race, Class, Gender, and the Dialectics of Liberation.*

22. (Eds.) Anderson, Kevin B. & Rockwell, Russell (2012). *The Dunayevskaya-Marcuse-Fromm Correspondence, 1954-1978: Dialogues on Hegel, Marx and Critical Theory*, Maryland: Lexington Books, p. 73.

Chapter 5

Ecology and Life in the Pandemic: Capital's Treadmill of Growth and Destruction

By Heather A. Brown

Report to the July 2020 Interim Convention of the International Marxist-Humanist Organization, slightly updated.

> *One basis for life and another for science is* a priori *a falsehood.*
>
> — Marx, *1844 Manuscripts*

The reality of life in 2020 is one of overlapping crises—Covid-19, a deep economic recession, climate change and its related effects, and the dehumanization of persons of color, just to name a few. All of these and more are fundamentally related to attempts by capital to despotically control all of nature, including human beings for the purpose of extracting whatever surplus value it can. This despotic control has reached a point where it can be said without exaggeration that capital has become hostile to the continuance of life on Earth. This is especially clear in the case of the ecological crisis that capitalism faces and in one of its most pressing recent manifestations, Covid-19.

Earlier this year as wildfires raged across Australia at an unprecedented rate, seeming to signal an urgency in preventing further climate change, many in the world paid lip service to the threatening ecological crisis that is clear to soon envelop the world in catastrophic change—rising temperatures, glacial melting, rising sea levels, increasing drought in some regions, loss of biodiversity, increasing scarcity of clean water, etc. Earth's average temperature has increased about 1.6 degrees Fahrenheit (0.9 degrees Celsius) since the late 19th century, most of which has occurred in the past 35 years, with the six warmest years on record taking place since 2014. Globally, sea levels rose about eight inches (about 20 cm) in the 20th century and we are currently on track to double that this century.[1] Scientists predict that the effects on human communities will be profound and will likely include temperature increases which could by 2070 rise to levels that will make about 19% of the Earth unhabitable by humans;[2] droughts in many parts of the world that will disrupt local and international food chains, leading to at the very least, regional famines; increasing water shortages that could lead to regional conflict; increased transmission of infectious disease; and the flooding and submersion of low-lying coastal areas. All of the above are likely to increase conflict as well as create new climate refugees seeking basic survival. Moreover, those who will likely see the greatest negative effects of climate change are those least able to mitigate those effects due to poverty among many other factors.

How Did We Get Here?

The basic story of climate change is a familiar and (outside of the far-right) a non-controversial truth. The increased use of fossil fuels since the Industrial Revolution has led to atmospheric degradation. These fossil fuels, which took thousands of years to create, have been burned for their energy and released into the atmosphere at an alarming rate. With more carbon dioxide, methane and other greenhouse gases in the atmosphere, the Earth has been getting warmer since greenhouse gases reduce the amount of heat that can escape the atmosphere into space.

---

1. See more at "Climate Change: How Do We Know?" Accessible here: https://climate.nasa.gov/evidence/

2. Regan, Helen "Billions of People Could Live in Areas Too Hot for Humans by 2070, Study Says" in *CNN*, May 6, 2020. Accessible here: https://edition.cnn.com/2020/05/05/world/global-warming-climate-niche-temperatures-intl-hnk/index.html

While the above is relatively uncontroversial, there are at least two prominent theories of why humans have caused climate change. One argues that the current age is one of the Anthropocene, meaning that human beings as such are having a large enough effect on the climate to represent an entire era of environmental history. In brief, this theory is problematic as it posits abstract human beings outside of any particular mode of production as the cause of climate change. This theory follows the logic of capitalism which argues that human beings have always been egoistic and acquisitive and rules out the possibility of a different type of social relations as human nature is unchanging and unchangeable.

Others such as Jason Moore would argue that the current environmental regime is one of the Capitalocene. Here, it is the relations inherent in capitalism, in its incessant drive to attain greater and greater surplus value which leads to the destruction of the environment. While space prevents a full discussion and critique of Moore's work, I would like to point out some of the most significant aspects of his understanding of the relationship between humanity and nature.[3] Perhaps the most noteworthy of these is his critique of the majority of left ecologists that either explicitly or implicitly maintain a theoretic separation between nature and society where each is nearly completely isolated from the other. Moore points in the direction of a theory that dialectically combines the interrelations between nature and culture which can be more useful. Here there are constant interactions between human beings and the natural world where it becomes impossible to completely separate the two. Human beings create new nature while simultaneously, nature acts on and

---

3. For a full theoretical exposition of this theory, see Moore, Jason W. (2015). *Capitalism and the Web of Life: Ecology and the Accumulation of Capital*, New York: Verso. For an interesting application of these theoretic premises, see Patel, Raj & Moore, Jason W. (2017). *A History of the World in Seven Cheap Things: A Guide to Capitalism, Nature, and the Future of the Planet*, Berkeley: University of California Press. Where Moore's argument is especially problematic is in his adherence to a theory of underconsumptionism which posits that capital must continually expand to non-capitalist realms in order to avoid and/or overcome economic crises, ignoring the importance of labor to capital as well as subjective possibilities. However, his is a more nuanced look at the issue than most which includes important discussions of gender and social reproduction, for example.

changes the human being.

As Kohei Saito (2017) rightly points out, Moore's theory is problematic in that he trades the Cartesian dualism of "nature" v. "culture" for an undifferentiated unity of the two. As Marx notes in numerous places in his work, humans are natural beings, but they are also unique in the sense that they are also conscious beings, capable of conscious change to their environment in a way that nature never can:

> A spider conducts operations which resemble those of the weaver, and a bee would put many a human architect to shame by the construction of its honeycomb cells. But what distinguishes the worst architect from the best of bees is that the architect builds the cell in his mind before he constructs it in wax. At the end of every labour process, a result emerges which had already been conceived by the worker at the beginning, hence already existed ideally. Man not only effects a change of form in the materials of nature; he also realizes his own purpose in those materials.[4]

If we do not maintain this conceptual distinction between the human being and nature, the subjective aspect of humanity cannot be understood, nor can purposeful change happen. Thus, Moore cuts off the most important avenue for humanity to overcome this crisis.[5] However, we do not need to follow Moore this far with his unitary theory. Instead, a dialectical unity of humanity and nature where both commonality and difference are acknowledged can be conceptualized. As Marx argued in the 18th Brumaire of Louis Bonaparte, "Men make their own history, but they do not make it just as they please in circumstances they choose for themselves; rather they make it in present circumstances, given and inherited."[6] The same can be said for nature as for history.

Another important point for Moore is that we must look closely

---

4. Marx, Karl (1976). *Capital: A Critique of Political Economy*, Vol. I, New York: Penguin. p. 284.

5. Saito, Kohei "Marx in the Anthropocene: Value, Metabolic Rift, and the Non-Cartesian Dualism" in *Zeitschrift für kritische Sozialtheorie und Philosophie*, No. 4 (1–2), 2017, pp. 276–295.

6. "The Eighteenth Brumaire of Louis Bonaparte" in (ed.) Carver, Terrell (1996). *Marx: Later Political Writings*, Cambridge: Cambridge University Press, p. 32.

at the relations between humanity and nature, not as such, but in social and historical context. Human beings do not interact with the natural world in the same way in a feudal society as they do in a capitalist society. Moreover, within different stages of capitalism, humanity's relationship with nature may shift. The reverse can also be true—climate conditions affect capitalist relations and the opportunities available for individual capitalists to expand. Looking at the issue from a more global perspective, we can perhaps say that contemporary capitalism has developed to the point where its own rapacious nature has led to conditions that further limit its ability to expand and survive (more on this below).

This type of thinking undermines the logic of neo-Malthusian environmentalists who would argue that overconsumption and an increasing world population are the biggest problems. Instead, the issue is that capitalism so exhausts the inputs of nature and the available labor power such that these workers and resources will not be able to reproduce themselves at the same rate, quality or cost for capital. It becomes more expensive for capitalists to do business, cutting the rate of surplus value. Simply reining in overconsumption through state interventions like population control, pollution regulation, or caps on production would, at best, slow down the degradation of nature, but could never solve it. Similarly, the proposed Green New Deal would be a positive development in the sense that it prioritizes new green technology, more democratic control of industry and a stronger social safety net. However, the basis of this program is a neo-Keynesianism which does not question the basis of capitalism itself, thus it cannot be effective in bringing about the type of transformative change necessary to stave off the climate crisis. Capital's raison d'etre is to expand its accumulation of value and the only way of doing this is through the exploitation of the "free gifts" of nature—i.e. overworked nature and human beings that cannot continue to reproduce themselves in the same way for future rounds of production—hence, the necessity of further degradation of the natural world.

Ecology, the Pandemic and Capital

The Covid-19 pandemic underlines the close relationship between capitalist relations and the natural world. It should be noted that this is far from an instance of "nature" reasserting itself against humanity. Instead, the very conditions for a pandemic are written into the social relations of globalized capitalism at a number of levels. Sonia Shah in *Pandemic: Tracking Contagions from Cholera to Ebola and Beyond* charts the outbreak of pandemics in the modern world starting with Cholera in the early 1800s. There had been outbreaks of Cholera in parts of India for a very long time, which could become a local epidemic, but not a large-scale pandemic. She argues that in part, what made the Cholera pandemic possible was the dense concentration of people together in cities, high levels of poverty coupled with inadequate sanitation, and the increased ability of individuals to travel throughout the world, spreading the disease. All of these factors were made possible by a particular type of social organization: capitalism. While it is very unlikely that Shah herself could be accused of being a socialist, she shines light on the degree to which capitalism in bringing parts of the world together through commerce, the increased agrarian production that allowed for more people to live and work in cities and through the vast inequality that value production creates, opened up significant ground for the possibility of pandemics.

Additionally, Shah is keen to point out that we are likely to see an increase in epidemics and pandemics. This has as much to do with social relations as it does with the biology of viruses. As we have seen with Covid-19, geography is no barrier to transmission. When it is possible to travel around the world by jet, cruise ship, train or car, securing borders from contagions is almost impossible, especially if there is little or no advance warning. Add to that the motive to sweep under the rug the outbreak of a new virulent pathogen as has been the case in countries like the US and China in order to protect tourism, industry and reputation, and you have a recipe for a full-scale world pandemic.

Moreover, because viruses can adapt to their environments in unique ways, the possibility of more virulent pathogens only increases as interactions among humans and between humans and animals increases. Viruses, bacteria and other microbes have the ability to acquire traits through horizontal gene transfer, meaning that as they interact with each other, they can pick up the traits of that microbe simply from that interaction. Antibiotic resistant MRSA emerged in this way, for example.[7] Thus, more interaction between live beings creates the possibility of more dangerous pathogens. This issue will certainly not be abated in the new society and, in fact, the interaction of people from all parts of the world may increase. What will be different, however, is that these and other interactions will not be driven by profit, but by socialized human needs. When epidemics or pandemics happen, there will be appropriate infrastructure in place to combat it such as free adequate and equal healthcare for all, PPE supplies on the basis of need instead of profit, public dissemination of factual information to a public that can critically assess this information, and scientific research that is driven by community interests rather than profit.

Finally, capital's drive to produce greater amounts of surplus value factor significantly into the equation. For example, the overuse of antibiotics on farm animals to maintain their health in the completely unhealthy conditions of factory farms has been common. Also, for reasons that are not fully understood scientifically, antibiotics help these animals grow faster, meaning less time between birth and slaughter—less cost of doing business and faster turnaround means a greater profit. This use of antibiotics has led to the development of antibiotic resistant pathogens that is making medical care more difficult and increasing the potential for even more lethal pandemics in the future.

While Covid-19 is a natural phenomenon in most senses, because it exists in a globalized capitalist world, it lays bare many of the contradictions of contemporary capitalism. It is certainly no accident that Black, Latinx and other persons of color are being disproportionately affected by Covid-19—in fact, the dualities of

---

7. Shah, Sonia (2016). *Pandemic: Tracking Contagions from Cholera to Ebola and Beyond*, New York: Sarah Crichton Books, Farrar, Straus and Giroux. p. 72.

capitalism and its understanding of "nature" and "society" as well as how it values these things has meant that there will always be workers and aspects of "nature" that will be disposable if it means greater profits for capital. Blacks are about 3.5 times more likely to die from Covid-19 and Latinx are twice as likely to die.[8] Native Americans make up 57% of cases and 72% of hospitalizations in New Mexico.[9] The Navajo Nation alone has had more cases of Covid-19 than 12 states and more deaths than 7 states.[10]

These disparities can be traced to a number of factors stemming from structural inequalities which have been legitimized through the implicit and explicit rhetoric of biological differences which have no real scientific legitimacy once environmental factors are brought in. These groups are not more likely to be diabetic, have heart disease, or asthma because of some genetic predisposition as the medical community often presumes, instead capital has deemed these groups disposable and has naturalized their eventual deaths from these environmental factors.

Take for example, the prevalence of asthma and cancer within minority communities, which are also significant risk factors for complications from Covid-19. A recent study found that Blacks and Latinx breathe much dirtier air that contains PM2.5 particles—extremely small particulates that can collect in the lungs and lead to cancer and other lung problems. Blacks are exposed to 56% more pollution than caused by their consumption and Latinx are exposed to 63%. For non-Hispanic

---

8. Hathaway, Bill "New analysis quantifies risk of COVID-19 to racial, ethnic minorities" in *Yale News*, May 19, 2020. Accessible here: https://news.yale.edu/2020/05/19/new-analysis-quantifies-risk-covid-19-racial-ethnic-minorities

9. Kaplan, Elise & Davis, Theresa "'Huge Disparity' in COVID-19 death rates for Native Americans in NM" in *Alberquerque Jounal*, May 30, 2020. Accessible here: https://www.abqjournal.com/1461218/huge-disparity-in-covid19-death-rates-for-native-americans-in-nm.html

10. DeSantis, Rachel "Navajo Nation Has More COVID-19 Cases Than 12 States — and More Deaths Than 7 States Combined" in *People*, June 11, 2020. Accessible here: https://people.com/human-interest/navajo-nation-more-covid-cases-7-states-combined/

whites, they are exposed to 17% less than their consumption.[11]

Similarly, there have been disproportionate deaths by race in Louisiana. Some of this can be linked to what is known as "Cancer Alley." This is an 85-mile area between New Orleans and Baton Rouge that is home to more than 150 chemical plants and refineries. This area has seen five times higher death rates from Covid-19 than the rest of the nation. A recent study from Harvard showed a strong relationship between exposure to PM2.5 particles and Covid-19 deaths even after other factors were controlled for such as healthcare access, poverty, unemployment, and preexisting conditions.[12]

These are just two of many examples of how capitalist-led environmental destruction has put minority communities at greater risk of disease and death. Easily added to these issues are safe water issues on Native American reservations, unsafe water in many cities due to failing infrastructure, food deserts, and the greater heat exposure of cities.[13] These seemingly natural problems become social and changeable problems when viewed as what they really are: the result of capitalism's efforts to eke out surplus value from nature—whether that is via a static ahistorically created human

---

11. Rice, Doyle "Study Finds Race Gap in Air Pollution—Whites Largely Cause It, Blacks and Hispanics Breath It" in *USA Today*, March 12, 2019. Accessible here: https://www.usatoday.com/story/news/nation/2019/03/11/air-pollution-inequality-minorities-breathe-air-polluted-whites/3130783002/

12. Ramirez, Rachel "A Tale of Two Crises: Wake-Up Call: As coronavirus ravages Louisiana, 'cancer alley' residents haven't given up the fight against polluters" in *Grist*, May 4, 2020. Accessible here: https://grist.org/justice/as-coronavirus-ravages-louisiana-cancer-alley-residents-havent-given-up-the-fight-against-polluters/

13. A study in the journal Climate, found that "redlining" is a strong predictor of which neighborhoods are exposed to extreme heat. These neighborhoods are less likely to have green spaces and will contain more concrete and other materials that will trap heat due to the "heat island effect." "The analysis examined 108 urban areas across the country, and found that 94 percent of historically redlined neighborhoods are consistently hotter than the rest of the neighborhoods in their cities, underscoring a major environmental justice issue. Portland, Oregon, showed one of the largest heat disparities between redlined and non-redlined communities — up to 12.6 degrees F." Ramirez, Rachel "Another legacy of redlining: Unequal exposure to heat waves" in *Grist*, January 15, 2020. Accessible here: https://grist.org/justice/another-legacy-of-redlining-unequal-exposure-to-heat-waves/

being or a static ahistorical "natural" commodity. This is why it is so important to view nature and society as dialectically related rather than as simply isolated and opposing forces. Urban spaces and marginalized individuals are finally seen as not just existing outside history but are a part of capitalist nature that human beings have created. The natural becomes historical and thus changeable.

Moving Forward

Capitalism's defining feature is its need to create greater and greater amounts of surplus value. It can only do this successfully through commodification and its necessary movement of abstracting out all concrete characteristics other than an object's ability to produce surplus value. This is the only use value that capital truly acknowledges. Because of this, it makes no difference to the capitalist what is produced, how it is made or what harm comes from its production. The worker without health insurance who becomes sick can be replaced by another who is healthy at the same or potentially lower rate. The chicken that is genetically engineered in such a way that it can barely stand upright because of its large breasts is more commercially profitable,[14] and thus, better than the non-genetically modified chicken. Neither the fate of the worker or the chicken matters to capital.

This illustrates the need to uproot capitalism. It is a cruel system that can never work for human or natural interests as its sole purpose is to continually produce. A supply of one good is totally consumed, so it is then time to look to a new source of surplus value. Capitalism's rapacious nature is such that it will continue to destroy the bases of life beyond the point where it loses profitability. There is no hope that it can or will regulate itself.

We have recently seen the growth of celebrity Greta Thunberg and other young environmental activists who are calling for a change in the way in which human beings interact with the natural world through

---

14. Patel, Raj & Moore, Jason W. (2017). *A History of the World in Seven Cheap Things: A Guide to Capitalism, Nature, and the Future of the Planet*, Berkeley: University of California Press.

events like school strikes and Thunberg using her celebrity to get the message out that the status quo will destroy the planet. While not yet a Marxist movement, these efforts illustrate an important step forward as they show not only the negative of climate change, but also indicate that another world is possible. These young people who will have to disproportionately bear the burden of capital's frenzied activity to extract as much value as possible, have taken the first step of saying "no" to the current system and are just beginning to think about what an ecologically sustainable society might look like. Perhaps most encouraging is Thunberg's recent statements which seem to indicate that she is beginning to see the interconnected nature of capitalist oppression. For example, in discussing the Black Lives Matter Movement she says that society "passed a social tipping point, we can no longer look away from what our society has been ignoring for so long whether it is equality, justice or sustainability."[15] As she and many other young activists take to the streets and public airwaves demanding change, we should critically support their message and encourage them to think deeper about what a new society should look like.

Certainly, the Covid-19 crisis begins to show that another world is possible. Carbon emissions this year are estimated to be between 4.4-8% less than last year. This would be the lowest levels since World War II.[16] Wild animals have been seen roaming urban spaces devoid of people. These sorts of things show that we have not reached a point of no return, and that there is still time to avoid the worst, however, this reprieve is only temporary. It was the power of the state which forced business and industrial closures and mandated lockdowns for citizens in a time of crisis. These types of policies have already shown signs of wear perhaps most visibly with the recent armed protests in the Michigan State legislature. Individuals were essentially protesting

---

15. Rowlatt, Justin "Greta Thunberg: Climate Change 'As Urgent' as Coronavirus" in *BBC*, June 20, 2020. Accessible here: https://www.bbc.com/news/science-environment-53100800

16. Andrew, Scottie "Covid-19 Lockdowns Could Drop Carbon Emissions to Their Lowest Level Since World War II, but the Change May be Temporary" in *CNN*, May 19, 2020. Accessible here: https://www.cnn.com/2020/05/19/world/carbon-emissions-coronavirus-pandemic-scn-climate-trnd/index.html

for a return to normal—the right to be exploited by their bosses and the right to spread a deadly infection. Others, including prominent politicians have called for a reopening even at the expense of a greater death toll. For many, the system must be maintained at any cost, thus state-mandated change outside of a clear emergency is unlikely to be tolerated for long enough to do any real good.

Hence the importance of our work on *The Critique of the Gotha Program*. As Marx addresses the Gotha Program in his own era, we need to continue our work to theorize an alternative to capitalism which can bridge the gulf between "nature" and "society" in both theory and practice. This will involve great creative efforts from our organization and others of like minds in order to truly unite the purposes of the natural and social sciences in such a way that they are able to truly serve all regardless of race, class, gender, sexuality, gender identity, and ability. However, as Marx notes, the foundation has already been partially laid:

> But natural science has penetrated all the more practically into human life through industry. It has transformed human life and prepared the emancipation of humanity even though its immediate effect was to accentuate the dehumanization of man. Industry is the actual historical relationship of nature, and thus of natural science, to man. If industry is conceived as the exoteric manifestation of the essential human faculties, the human essence of nature and the natural essence of man can also be understood. Natural science will then abandon its abstract materialist, or rather idealist, orientation, and will become the basis of a human science, just as it has already become—though in an alienated form—the basis of actual human life. One basis for life and another for science is a priori a falsehood. Nature, as it develops in human history, in the act of genesis of human society, is the actual nature of man; thus nature, as it develops through industry, though in an alienated form, is truly anthropological nature.[17]

---

17. Karl Marx. 2004. The Economic and Philosophic Manuscripts of 1844, in Erich Fromm, ed., Marx's Concept of Man. New York: Continuum.

Chapter 6

Battle of Ideas: Responding to the New World of COVID-19, Economic Crisis, and Anti-Racist Uprisings

By Kevin B. Anderson

Adapted from a presentation to the July 2020 Interim Convention of the International Marxist-Humanist Organization.

This spring, as some countries began to reopen after months of COVID-19 lockdowns, youthful rebellions broke out inside the two most powerful states in the world, the USA and China. The Black youth of Minneapolis, their allies, and countless others across the USA expressed their anger on the streets over yet another police murder, which was one too many. During the same days, the youth of Hong Kong renewed their protests against new anti-democratic moves by the Chinese government. The US protests, which grew into a massive nationwide Black Lives Matter uprising, also had a major international impact. In both cases, the USA and China, the youth did not flinch in the face of brutal police repression, inspiring their elders and many others around the world. These youth face a world of mass unemployment, precipitous economic inequality, and growing racial oppression fueled by rightwing populism, all of it worsened by COVID-19 and the economic meltdown. This is a world they did not make and that they refuse to inhabit as passive objects. What are the roots of the situation facing us in the year 2020? And what is the way out? In the ensuing discussion, I will begin with the underlying systemic, i.e., capitalist, social structures, before moving to the subjective responses of live human beings, both in revolutionary action and in theoretical preparation for such action.

Going Beneath Appearance: COVID-19 and the Essence of Capitalism

The abject failure of almost all governments around the world to deal with the COVID-19 pandemic is above all a crisis of capitalism, with the chaotic response of Trump's America its most repellent phenomenal form. But too narrow a focus on Trump obscures how this abject failure illustrates the essential nature of capitalism, its "normal" macabre workings, which are now revealed more openly. Capitalism's quest for limitless value creation — and profit — has itself been compared to a virus afflicting humanity. This is because capitalism puts everything else aside, exists for the moment, and destroys even the possibility of the reproduction of its own means of production — including its labor force — in the long run. This is the underlying explanation for the lack of medical supplies, of tests, of masks, let alone a real public health infrastructure ready to save humanity from the pandemics that are becoming more and more frequent.

From its earliest days, the capitalist system has been beset by chaotic production relations. In one sense, this leads to a total instability in workers lives, as they are thrown from overwork during boom times into mass unemployment during those crises that are endemic to the system. Even physical survival is always in question, as the unemployed can actually face starvation. As Karl Marx and Frederick Engels intone in the *Communist Manifesto* (1848) in an attack on the industrial bourgeoisie, the main wing of the ruling class under capitalism: "It is unfit to rule because it is incompetent to assure an existence to its slave within his slavery."[1] This is a unique feature of capitalism, even compared to earlier forms of class society. In these precapitalist class societies, tiny minorities already dominated the working people and extracted from them a surplus product, which kept the ruling class wealthy and underpinned a state to protect them. But at the same time, some precapitalist societies tried to allow the working people a minimum material existence, despite the low development of the productive forces at the time.

As Rosa Luxemburg noted more than a century ago with regard to

---

1. Marx, Karl & Engels, Friedrich (1975). *Marx-Engels Collected Works: Vol. 6*, New York: International Publishers, p. 495.

British rule in India, imperialism under capitalism is unique in that it actually drains society dry, failing even to put enough of its profits into preserving its very means of exploitation:

Finally, the specifically capitalist method of colonization finds expression in the following striking circumstance. The British were the first conquerors of India to show a gross indifference toward the works of civilization that formed its public utilities and economic infrastructure. Arabs, Afghans and Mongols alike had initiated and maintained magnificent works of canalization, they provided the country a network of roads, built bridges across rivers and sunk wells.... 'The Company that ruled India until 1858 (the East India Company — R.L.) did not make one spring accessible, did not sink a single well, nor build a bridge for the benefit of the Indians.'[2]

While wages and living conditions — then and now — might be better in Western Europe or North America than in India, the basic framework is the same, that of capitalist exploitation, even to the point of draining life itself from the working people. And under capitalist slavery, Black people were literally worked to death, which led Marx to write that, even compared to Roman times, slavery reached "its most hateful form ... in a situation of capitalist production."[3]

If slavery was the most brutal form of exploitation under capitalism, in *Capital* Marx also writes of the slow death of the working class in industrialized Britain. He compares the rule of capital to the domination of a Juggernaut, a vehicle that crushes spectators beneath it in a religious festival, in what amounts to a human sacrifice:

Within the capitalist system all methods for raising the social productiveness of labour are brought into effect at the cost of the individual laborer; that all means for the development of production undergo a dialectical inversion so that they become means of domination and exploitation of the producers; they distort the worker into a fragment of a human being [*Teilmenschen*], they degrade him to the level of an appendage of a machine, ...subject him

---

2. Luxemburg, Rosa "The Accumulation of Capital: A Contribution to the Economic Theory of Imperialism" in (eds.) Hudis, Peter & Le Blanc, Paul (2016). *The Complete Works of Rosa Luxemburg, Vol. 2: Economic Writings*, Brooklyn: Verso, p. 270.

3. Marx, Karl & Engels, Friedrich (1975). *Marx-Engels Collected Works: Vol. 30*, New York: International Publishers, p. 197.

during the labour process to a despotism the more hateful for its meanness; they transform his life-time into working-time, and drag his wife and child beneath the wheels of the Juggernaut of capital.[4]

How true that rings at a time when US workers — mainly superexploited Latinx immigrants — are being forced back to work in meatpacking plants that are rife with COVID-19. Not only that. White rightwing mobs also applaud, guns in hand, the idea of going back to work, literally calling for human sacrifices on the altar of capital, all in order to "get the economy moving again."

Going Beyond Essence 1: Imagining an Alternative to Capitalism

At best, most radical analysis stops here, at exposing the underlying essence of capitalism, but it is important to go beyond essence to subject, to the possibility of revolutionary change. It is so hard to imagine an alternative to capitalism that it is sometimes helpful, as Marx also does in *Capital*, to refer to "other forms of production."[5] But here I would like to go beyond the text of *Capital* to one of Marx's very last writings, the *Ethnological Notebooks*. In these 1880–82 notes on a variety of non-European societies, he records a description of an Indigenous communist society in the Americas that operates exactly the opposite of capitalism, producing a surplus product that is not surplus value and that is geared not to the reproduction of capital or the riches of a ruling class, but rather to the security and reproduction of life:

> Rev. Sam. Gorman, missionary with the Laguna Pueblo Indians, in address to the Historical Society of New Mexico says: 'The right of property belongs to the female part of the family, and descends in that line from mother to daughter. Their land is held in common, but after a person cultivates a lot he has personal claim to it, which he can sell to one of the community... Their women, generally, have control of the granary, are more provident than their Spanish neighbors about the future. Ordinarily they try to have a

---

4. Marx, Karl (1976). *Capital: A Critique of Political Economy, Vol. 1* (Ben Fowkes's translation), New York: Penguin, p. 799.

5. Ibid, p. 169.

year's provision on hand. It is only when two years of scarcity succeed each other, that Pueblos, as a community, suffer hunger.'[6]

Note that in this communistic Indigenous society women retain significant social power, not only over the land, but also over the social reproduction of food. As a result, this technologically underdeveloped society was "more provident than its Spanish neighbors," let alone 21st century capitalism, which can't even prepare for the epidemics its own scientists predict.

Similarly, in the *Critique of the Gotha Program*, Marx theorizes a first phase of communism, where workers would not receive the "full proceeds" of their labor because of the need for "common funds" to sustain the community:

> He receives a certificate from society that he has furnished such-and-such an amount of labor (after deducting his labor for the common funds); and with this certificate, he draws from the societal supply of means of consumption as much as the same amount of labor cost.

This is from our new translation (by Karel Ludenhoff and me), which I am proud to report will appear as a book with PM Press next year, with Peter Hudis's introduction. That modern kind of communism Marx was theorizing would also, as in his description of the achievements of the Paris Commune of 1871, get "rid of the standing army and the police, the physical force elements of the old Government."[7]

Marx also suggests that more traditional and more modern kinds of communist organization of social life — here mentioning the longstanding communism of the Russian village community and the kind of modern communism he theorized in *Critique of the Gotha Program* and that the Western European proletariat yearned for — could link up as part of a revolutionary process. This is seen in his last published writing, the preface to the 1882 Russian edition of the *Communist Manifesto*: "If the Russian Revolution becomes the signal for a proletarian revolution in the West, so that both complement each other, the present Russian common ownership of land may serve as

---

6. Marx, Karl (1974). *Ethnological Notebooks*, Assen: Van Gorcum, p. 118.

7. "Civil War in France" in Marx, Karl & Engels, Friedrich (1986). *Marx-Engels Collected Work: Vol. 22*, London: Lawrence & Wishart, p. 331.

the starting point for a communist development."[8] That, ultimately, is the solution to the kind of social crisis brought on by COVID-19.

COVID-19, Racism, and Modern State-Capitalism

As discussed above, the COVID-19 pandemic is a capitalist crisis because capitalism is a form of society that does very little to secure the lives and health of the working people in its ruthless, limitless, and utterly impersonal drive for value creation.

But the pandemic is a capitalist crisis in a second sense. The actual destruction of human existence as a possibility is a product of the third and hopefully final stage of global capitalism, state-capitalism, which followed the competitive and then the monopoly stage, with the latter self-destructing during the Great Depression of the 1930s. First, we have seen how the Great Depression and the transformation into opposite of the Russian revolution created the basis for two forms of totalitarian state-capitalism, Nazi Germany and Stalinist Russia, each of which killed tens of millions of people in their concentration camps, mainly workers and peasants. Hitler's death camps gave the world a new, horrific word to describe his eliminationist anti-Semitism, "genocide." That genocide has repeated itself, most tragically in Rwanda, Central Africa in the 1990s. Second, we have seen how state-capitalism — here in the form of the somewhat progressive Roosevelt administration during World War 2 — created the nuclear weapons that still threaten the existence of most forms of life on the planet. Third, we have seen how, as levels of ecological destruction escalate, state-capitalism threatens utterly to destroy human and many other forms of life on the planet.

To these we can now add a fourth form of state-capitalism's death grip on humanity, global pandemics that threaten human existence. As shown by science journalist Sonia Shah in her 2016 book, *Pandemic*, more frequent, more virulent, and more deadly epidemics have been

---

8. (Ed.) Shanin, Theodor (1983). *Late Marx and the Russian Road*, New York: Monthly Review Press Classics, p. 139.

predicted by scientists for decades. Modern state-capitalism destroys the habitat of many animals, bringing them and the diseases they carry into closer contact with humans. Modern state-capitalism also engages in the capture, trade, and global transport of a wide variety of "exotic" animals, bringing all kinds of species into close contact with each other and with human beings for the first time, allowing diseases to spring from species to species, acquiring greater virulence. At a more general level, modern state-capitalism is the most globalized form of capitalism ever, thus facilitating its wide and rapid spread. While each of these forms of destruction threaten to wipe out much of humanity, they also have a class and racist basis, in that the poorest and most oppressed are the most vulnerable.

The Current Economic Crisis

The pandemic is a crisis of capitalism in a third major sense, in that it has touched off the greatest economic downturn since the 1930s. Capitalist ideologues of all stripes are working feverishly to perpetuate the fiction that the current economic crisis is only temporary (rightwingers), or that it will be more permanent (liberals and progressives), but that in either case the it is caused by COVID-19. This is a remarkably narrow notion of causality. For example, while the Minneapolis uprising was sparked by the racist police murder of George Floyd, even the liberal mayor referred in his speech both to longstanding issues of brutality and racism in the police department and to 400 years of slavery and oppression of Black people in the USA.

Why is it so hard to see something like this with the economic crisis sparked by COVID-19? And for those on the left who see these capitalist roots, why do they so often limit their critique to neoliberalism rather than capitalism as such?[9] Our Convention Call details the underlying stagnation of the US and the global economy: GDP growth in the US has been tepid, only 2.3% in 2019, and as we also wrote, "The economic growth that occurred prior to COVID-19

---

9. See, for example, Alfredo Saad-Filho, "From Covid-19 to the End of Neoliberalism," *Critical Sociology*, 2020

clearly was insufficient to reverse growing social inequality."[10] Despite the ballyhooed decrease in the official unemployment rate in the past couple of years in the U.S., this number does not count those too discouraged to seek work.

Another statistic that counts better those discouraged workers is the civilian labor force participation rate, i.e., the percentage of adults employed or actively seeking work. It has steadily declined over the past two decades in the USA. In April 2000 it stood at 67.3% of the working age population, but plunged to 64.6% by September 2013, in the wake of the Great Recession. Had the U.S. recovered from that recession in the way it was touted by Trump and the media, the labor force participation rate would have gone back up toward 2000 levels by 2020. It did not. Instead, on the eve of the pandemic in February 2020 it had actually declined slightly from 2013, to 63.4%, another clear indication of economic stagnation in the midst of supposed nearly full employment. Now, of course, it is in free fall.[11] Thus, the economic crisis touched off by the pandemic — and based in part on longterm economic stagnation — is just that, a real economic crisis from which no quick recovery can be expected. As our Call also states, "In a word, stagnation rules the day. This did not result from the coronavirus; that was instead its proximate cause. Capitalism has been producing a lot of rotten fruit that was just waiting to fall."

Thus, the current situation of pandemic and economic collapse is the product of capitalist social relations in three major ways: (1) It reveals capitalism's pursuit of surplus value at any cost, with a reckless disregard for the safety of the working people it exploits, rather than just the failings of neoliberalism. (2) Global pandemics like COVID-19 will occur more frequently under the most advanced form of capitalism, state-capitalism, which has also produced genocide,

10. Anderson, Kevin B.; Hudis, Peter; Johansson, Jens; Ludenhoff, Karel & Monzó, Lilia D. "Where to Begin? Growing Seeds of Liberation in a World Torn Asunder" in *The International Marxist-Humanist*, April 10, 2020. Accessible here: https://imhojournal.org/articles/where-to-begin-growing-seeds-of-liberation-in-a-world-torn-asunder/

11. US Bureau of Labor Statistics "Civilian Labor Force Participation Rate" June 4, 2020. Accessible here: https://www.bls.gov/charts/employment-situation/civilian-labor-force-participation-rate.htm

nuclear weapons, and unprecedented ecological destruction. (3) The pandemic was only the immediate cause of the economic depression, in a world economy already ripe for a crisis even deeper than the Great Recession of 2008.

Beyond Essence 2: Movements of Opposition and Liberation in the Year 2020[12]

Where does all this leave those striving for a world free of impoverishment and exploitation, of alienation and dehumanization, and of war, racism, sexism, heterosexism and environmental destruction? In one sense, we have been reeling over the past few months, locked down at home or forced to work in dangerous situations. During the lockdown, the world economy plummeted, throwing billions out of work. In India, low-wage workers have faced starvation. Some three billion people around the world lack access to water for the kind of handwashing public health officials deem necessary to mitigate the spread of COVID-19. Even in one of the richest cities in the world, Geneva, Switzerland, people lined up for a mile to receive a food donation toward the end of May.

Nonetheless, working people and youth have fought back in major ways during COVID-19 and the economic crisis. From the beginning, workers resisted attempts by capital and the state to keep production going, endangering their very lives. Here, the Italian workers, with their long militant tradition, led the way, with mass strike actions. In March, according to a report from CGIL, the main union federation:

> From the Dalmine steel mills of Bergamo to those of Brescia, from the Fiat-Chrysler plants of Pomigliano in Naples to the Ilva steel plant in Genoa, from the Electrolux factory of Susegana in Treviso to many small and medium-sized companies in Veneto and Emilia Romagna, from the Amazon warehouses in the provinces of Piacenza and Rieti, to the poultry

---

12. An earlier version of this section was published in my article "Notes on the Black Lives Matter Uprising in Historical and Global Context" in *The International Marxist-Humanist*, June 12, 2020. Accessible here: https://imhojournal.org/ articles/notes-on-the-black-lives-matter-uprising-in-historical-and-global-context/

and meat processing companies in the Po Valley, there were thousands of striking workers who came out into the squares and streets, strictly at a safe distance of one meter apart from each other, as prescribed by the government decree."[13]

This forced the state and capital to concede, leading to better safety measures and for workers to be paid during safety-related work stoppages.

These measures, aimed at unionized workers, did not affect the most precarious and marginalized workers, many of them immigrants. It was from this kind of milieu in the USA, the oppressed Black communities of Houston and Minneapolis, that George Floyd, murdered by four Minneapolis police, emerged. Like so many Black working class women and men, Floyd was semi-unemployed due to COVID-19 at the time that police choked him to death in slow motion, in broad daylight as witnesses from the Black community looked on and pleaded for mercy. Floyd's unconcscionable death has been seen as a form of lynching, but it also recalls the torture and executions carried out for centuries inside US slave plantations, where the audience was other enslaved people, and the purpose was to create dread by "making an example" of someone.

As many have also pointed out, the strangulation of George Floyd needs to be seen in the context of 400 years of slavery and the obdurate objective structures of racial oppression in the USA, from outright slavery, to Jim Crow, to today's mass incarceration. The poison of racism oozes through the sectors of employment, housing, education, healthcare, and policing, among others. Racialized capitalism in the US actually began under British colonialism as part of their widely-used policy of "divide and rule," from Ireland, to the Indian subcontinent, to Virginia. That strategy favored one sector of the populace against another, in order to prevent class unity against the rulers. In seventeenth-century Virginia, this meant arming poor but formally free whites and giving them police power over all

---

13. Tartaglia, Leopoldo "Dispatch from Italy: Class Struggle in the Time of Coronavirus" in *Labor Notes*, March 20, 2020. Accessible here: https://labornotes.org/2020/03/dispatch-italy-class-struggle-time-coronavirus?fbclid=IwAR39Rm Rqc54k8akyYwNGcD2gI1u8pL6fX5Tp7mZ_qIzn1vNfZI5DisKIPHM

Black people, the vast majority of them enslaved, in order to prevent another outbreak uniting white and Black labor, as had occurred in Bacon's rebellion in 1676. Today's police forces originate in part in the white militias that received rewards for capturing fugitive slaves.

But the racial history of the USA needs to be understood subjectively as much as objectively, in short, dialectically, if we are fully to grasp the current juncture. For today's rebellion on the streets can also trace itself to that uprising in early Virginia. In this sense, US history needs to be grasped as one of constant revolt and resistance in the face of racial and capitalist oppression. Here, one could mention (1) the slave revolts led by Denmark Vesey (1822) and Nat Turner (1831), (2) the whole period of Abolitionism, Civil War, and Reconstruction from the 1830s to the 1870s, (3) the southern rural Black Populists and their white allies in the 1890s, (4) the massive and socially progressive Black nationalist Garvey Movement after World War 1, (5) the mass interracial labor and Civil Rights movements of the 1930s, (6) the Civil Rights and Black liberation movements of the 1950s throughout the 1970s, and (7) the current period exemplified by the Sanders campaign against economic inequality and the development of Black Lives Matter, which preceded even the 2016 Sanders campaign, into a mass movement this spring that has drawn hundreds of thousands into the streets.

Today, as with the greatest of those previous movements, the Black masses have taken a vanguard role, but a wider movement has emerged involving youth of all races. As so many times before, the rulers and their representatives have tried to distinguish between "good" protestors and "illegal," "violent," and "outside" ones. Thus, after the mass rebellion against police brutality in 1965 in the Black ghetto of Watts, Los Angeles, some tried to blame "Cuban agents," but even the official McCone Commission led by a former head of the CIA could find none. Similarly, today's far-right Trump administration blames leftwing agitators from the Antifa movement, although they can show no concrete examples. What *is* true is that hundreds of thousands came onto the streets all across the country under the slogan "Black Lives Matter," that a police station was burned to the ground in Minneapolis, and that luxury shops in the Los Angeles area were attacked by protestors who scrawled slogans like "eat the rich" on walls. After over a week of rebellious actions across the land, all four Minneapolis police murderers were finally arrested, but this came after no less than 13,000 protestors had been detained.

The protests deepened and persisted in a way not seen since the 1960s. The Black Lives Matter Uprising has already developed into a nodal point, with facts on the ground demanding that any serious revolutionary analysis take these events as its starting point, as the beginning of a new revolutionary era with global dimensions.

Demonstrators were cruelly gassed and clubbed near the White House by direct presidential command, in order for Trump to show "toughness" at a photo op after it had been reported he was cowering in the basement. Even Trump's threat to use the regular army on the streets did not deter the demonstrators, but it did cause dissension within the military leadership, especially after it was reported that officials had used the term "dominating the battle space." As even retired General Martin Dempsey noted in protest, the law and military tradition restrict the use of such tactics to foreign enemies. But it is equally true that two decades of endless war abroad, of occupation and torture of civilians in Iraq and elsewhere, is blowing back into the USA itself, with police forces that are militarized as never before. Another form of blowback can be seen in how Minneapolis police have received training from the US-funded occupation police force of one of the most reactionary powers in the world, Netanyahu's Israel, where chokeholds and other "physical pressure," i.e., torture, of Palestinian detainees is totally legal. These facts show that moves in the USA toward an authoritarian state are not limited to the Trump administration, but can also be found in liberal Minneapolis. It also underlines the need to amend our Statement of Principles in the Constitution, to include this stronger language in support of Palestine: "We have always opposed Israel's oppressive policies against the Palestinians and strongly support their right to an independent and territorially viable state. At the same time, we oppose all forms of anti-Semitism and support the Jewish people's right to self-determination."

Less noticed but also extremely significant has been the

resurgence of the youth movement in Hong Kong against Chinese government attempts to extinguish all democratic rights in that semi-autonomous city. As the threat of COVID-19 lifted a bit, the youth of Hong Kong were the first anywhere in the world to reassert their pre-COVID movement on a truly mass scale. Inside China, quieter dissent exists amid deepening repression, especially in Wuhan, where the regime covered up the full extent of COVID-19 for weeks, thus extending the suffering in China and the world. On June 4, the 31st anniversary of the crushing of the China-wide student and worker uprising of 1989, tens of thousands of Hong Kong youth gathered for the annual commemoration, despite the event having been banned due to COVID-19. Thwarted by popular protest in their attempts to get a series of repressive measures through the Hong Kong legislature, China's top leader, Xi Jinping, has decided to act directly, an extremely ominous turn. It should also be noted that the Hong Kong protests have never been only about political issues, as residents also face a precipitous increase in economic inequality, as investment capital from the rest of China has led to skyrocketing rents and other forms of heightened capitalist oppression. For its part, while some governments have issued verbal protests, unelected global capital is solidly backing Xi's repressive measures, with all due cynicism: "There will be some unhappy people for some time," said John L. Thornton, a former president of Goldman Sachs who has close ties with the Chinese regime, "But the drum rolls, the dogs bark and the caravan moves on. That's the political judgment."[14] Thornton's racist comparison of the Chinese people to dogs should also be noted.

Contradictions on the Road Toward Liberation: Stalinism and Maoism's Betrayals of the Black Liberation Struggle

This year marks the 150th anniversary of the birth of V.I. Lenin, one of history's most important Marxists. Despite some serious

---

14. Quoted in Stevenson, Alexandra & Wang, Vivian "Why China May Call the World's Bluff on Hong Kong" in *The New York Times*, June 4, 2020.

flaws — the elitist vanguard party to lead and the single-party state he and Trotsky established after the revolution — Lenin propagated to the world the notion that without revolutionary theory there can be no revolutionary movement. This was of course in the spirit of Marx himself, who completed *Capital* at the height of one of his most active periods of engagement with the workers' movement, that of the First International. But what does it mean to develop revolutionary theory today in the wake of the myriad crises — and opportunities — facing us in the year 2020?

Writing in the wake of the 1960s, our founder Raya Dunayevskaya wrote of the need for revolutionaries to become philosophers of revolution. Posed at such a general level, many diverse socialists and radicals would agree. But once one looks deeper, key differences with Marxist-Humanism become clearer. In *Philosophy and Revolution* (1973), Dunayevskaya writes of two pitfalls to avoid, here debating about the African Revolutions of the 1960s, not with reformists, but genuine revolutionaries:

> We must, however, beware of falling into traps set by mechanical materialists as well as voluntarists, by ideologues rooted in other 'civilizations' as well as free-lancers. Although they call themselves Marxists, the vulgar materialists attribute an iron mold to economic laws...: they 'must' be sucked into the world market. The seeming opposite of vulgar materialists, the voluntarists — Maoists or individualists, Existentialists or anarchists — have one thing in common with those who are overwhelmed by economic laws: they believe they can order the workers to make 'one day equal twenty years.'[15]

What Dunayevskaya is critiquing here are the two dominant forms of Marxist socialism of the twentieth century.

What does this mean for today, especially for those like us who talk of race, class, and revolution? The vulgar materialists, found among both Russian Stalinists and Western European social democrats, tended toward class and economic reductionism, which under Stalinism became tied to the interests of the Soviet Union as the supposed representative of the revolutionary class at a global level.

---

15. Dunayevskaya, Raya (2015). *Philosophy and Revolution: From Hegel to Sartre, and from Marx to Mao*, Delhi: Aakar Books, pp. 218–19.

This was the ultimate form of class reductionism, where the interests of the class were themselves reduced to those of the USSR. This led to the infamous example of the Popular Front during the Second World War, when the global Communist Parties basically dropped their anti-racist demands for what they called anti-fascist unity. Thus, when African Americans sought to march on Washington in 1943 to end segregation in the U.S. military, the Stalinist US Communist Party denounced it as a divisive weakening of the anti-fascist effort.[16] Even in South Africa, nothing was supposed to be done against the white rulers. Since the Stalinists had long advocated Black liberation alongside the liberation of labor and had gained significant Black support, this betrayal struck deep, playing no small part in the disillusionment with all forms of Marxism after World War 2.

If the vulgar and rationalist materialism of the Stalinists and social democrats usually meant asking Blacks to wait for economic or political conditions to "mature," the Maoist split from Stalinism was more voluntaristic and sometimes even irrationalist, stressing the revolutionary will, that U.S. imperialism was a "paper tiger," etc. This stress on "daring" to struggle attracted many youths from the 1960s, including those around the Black Panther Party and the League of Revolutionary Black Workers in Detroit. Mao attacked the USSR as in league with U.S. imperialism, and noted how the French Communist Party had helped save the state's effort to blunt the near-revolution of 1968 by channeling it into reformist electoral politics. This also gained him intellectual followers like Jean-Paul Sartre, Simone de Beauvoir, and Michel Foucault. But Maoist opposition to this kind of reformism, and to Russia's often opportunistic aid to Third World liberation movements, led to a politics that placed opposition to Russia over everything, including Black liberation. In so doing, Mao's China cruelly betrayed African revolutionaries, especially in Southern Africa in the 1970s. For example, since Russia was giving some support to the main African liberation movement in Angola, China actually aligned itself with rightwing Angolan

---

16. See our co-founder Charles Denby's *Indignant Heart: A Black Worker's Journal* and also Ralph Ellison's classic novel *Invisible Man* which captures this period in fictionalized form.

forces opposing that movement. These forces were in fact allied with apartheid South Africa, which sent in troops to aid them. In a surprise move that exposed and thwarted this betrayal, Russia flew tens of thousands of Cuban troops to Angola at the invitation of the new liberationist government. They drove the South African racists back home. This led to another great disillusionment with Marxism on the part of Black people, especially the many who had leaned toward Maoism in that period and had been sympathetic to groups like the Panthers or the League. This was felt in intellectual circles as well, as many Black intellectuals moved away from Marxism.

Today, little of this heritage appears before us directly, although there are exceptions like Angela Davis's wrong-headed signature on a petition supporting the Iranian regime during the protests last fall. There is also a small resurgence of Maoism among today's youthful revolutionaries. More generally, the philosophical legacies of Stalinism and Maoism — whether in class reductionism or in the voluntaristic politics of the revolutionary will — can be found in many political movements and tendencies of today, as seen in some forms of "democratic socialism," of anarchism, or of Antifa.

The Future of the International Marxist-Humanist Organization: Toward the Dialectics of Organization

If we can recognize these problems and if we can instead espouse and continue to develop Marxist-Humanism, where does that leave us as an organization? Surely, we don't want to be simply critics and gadflies and we want to the best of our abilities to participate in, learn from, and help give positive direction to movements for human liberation. To be sure, we can offer these movements a deeper and more humanist theoretical perspective than most of them can develop spontaneously.

But what about ourselves as IMHO, our structure and our practice of our Marxist-Humanist principles? Does membership mean merely intellectual adherence to Marxist-Humanist principles and then working inside other movements as individuals? If so, then our organization could take the form of study groups or study circles that might have some vague or indirect influence on the wider movement. That could preserve and develop Marxist-Humanist ideas somewhat, but would it be a real organization?

Here, Lenin can assist us, via Dunayevskaya, who appreciated Lenin's concept of organizational membership as not just adhering to principles or paying your dues, but active participation in a group involving more than intellectuals in a study group. As Dunayevskaya writes in *Marxism and Freedom* (1958), much of Lenin's 1902 book *What Is to Be Done?* was derived from Karl Kautsky's notion that Marxist intellectuals were the real leaders of the working class, which could not arrive at socialist consciousness without them. Dunayevskaya meant this as a critique of Lenin. This is the elitist core of "vanguardism" and it needs to be critiqued strongly by us, as it has been.

But Dunayevskaya adds, crucially:

> There was an element in Lenin's theory on organization which was not borrowed from the German Social Democracy, which was specifically Leninist — the conception of what constitutes membership in a Russian Marxist group. Indeed, the definition did not merely rest on a 'phrase' — that only he is a member who puts himself 'under the discipline of the local organization.' The disciplining by the local was so crucial to Lenin's conception that it held primacy over verbal adherence to Marxist theory, propagandizing Marxist views, and holding a membership card.[17]

And that local, at least in Dunayevskaya's eyes, would if possible be comprised of working people, not just intellectuals and students, would be citywide, etc.

This point bears on our efforts to become a real organization that is not based solely on theoretical discussions, as important as they are. I'm not suggesting that we go back to Lenin's model, or even that of News and Letters Committees and its locals during Dunayevskaya's lifetime, as we have a wider, international organization now. But the valid point Lenin makes should not be lost because of this. It is also elucidated in his 1904 critique of the circle spirit. In addition, it bears on our ongoing critique of CLR James and others who advocated

---

17. Dunayevskaya, Raya (2000). *Marxism and Freedom: From 1776 until Today*, New York: Humanity Books, p. 180.

decentralized forms of organization in place of the vanguard party, but thought that the Marxist group should simply support and record the creativity of the mass movements, or theorize from the sidelines. What was lacking here was an organization that would truly link theory to practice, something the world needs more than ever today. As Dunayevskaya put it at the end of her life, in an addition to *Rosa Luxemburg, Women's Liberation, and Marx's Philosophy of Revolution*:

> This is the further challenge to the form of organization which we have worked out as the committee-form rather than the 'party-to-lead.' But, though committee-form and 'party-to-lead' are opposites, they are not absolute opposites. At the point when the theoretic-form reaches philosophy, the challenge demands that we synthesize not only the new relations of theory to practice, and all the forces of revolution, but philosophy's 'suffering, patience and labor of the negative,' i.e., experiencing absolute negativity.[18]

Thus, we seek to transcend/sublate (*Aufheben*) this duality between vanguardism and more decentralized forms of organization. This, comrades, is one of the main issues we need to grasp if we are to really develop as an organization rooted in the philosophy and principles of Marxist-Humanism. Doing so is not separate from developing ourselves theoretically, both individually and collectively, or from participating in, learning from, and grasping what is truly new in movements like the BLM Uprising. Rather, that process goes hand-in-hand with working out a new type of organization, one the world is crying out for but no one has developed, not even ourselves. However, we have at least posed the question.

---

18. Dunayevskaya, Raya (2015). *Rosa Luxemburg, Women's Liberation and Marx's Philosophy of Revolution*, Delhi: Aakar Books, p. xxxvii.

Chapter 7

Marxist-Humanism in the Heat of the Present

By Seamus Connolly

Presentation given at the International Marxist-Humanist Organization's 2020 Convention in July. Discusses the concept of a dialectical and revolutionary humanism and its relevance to the present moment.

On the Left today many look askance at humanism. They ridicule it, lambast it, and castigate it. And, in large swathes, they outlaw it and anyone who wishes to speak of it, neglecting in the process the diverse histories and multifarious traditions of humanism as living systems of thought and practice. Humanism has been many things, it is true: a fig-leaf justification for colonialism; a bourgeois denial of class politics; the belief in an abstract "Man" that squats outside of the world and that denies women, people of color, lesbians, gays, intersex, and disabled peoples the agency and affirmation of their particularity. But humanism has also been *the very basis of the attacks on these abominations*: from Marx to Dunayevskaya, Césaire to Fanon, Fromm to Kosík, and more. So, what, then, is humanism, considered in relation to Marxism, and why do we profess it?

Humanism and Human Value

All humanisms seek to elevate *human* value.[1] This elevation of human value is not carried out in the same way in each particular humanism, however (the history of liberal and bourgeois humanism

---

1. Roushui, Wang "A Defense of Humanism" in *Chinese Studies in Philosophy*, Vol. 16:3, 1985, pp. 71-88.

testifies to this), nor is it necessarily pursued at the expense of other types of value (such as the value that is represented in the life of non-human animals or in the health and vitality of the environment – both of which are related, in an intimate way, to human value). The elevation of human value is intrinsic to the Marxian project in that Marx's very critique of capital was *raised in the name of humanity*: the humanism that he announced in the *Economic and Philosophical Manuscripts* of 1844, and which Dunayevskaya rightly picked up and made the basis of the philosophy and practice of Marxist-Humanism, provided the initial and enduring motivation for his life's work in critiquing capital.

In seeking to demystify the alienation and fetishism of capitalist life, Marx raised the flag of *human* value as opposed to value in the sense of exchange value, that is to say, value in its economic sense. Through his analysis of value in political economy – which despite what is claimed by many Marxists today, is clearly inaugurated in the *Economic and Philosophical Manuscripts* – Marx unmasks the inversion whereby human value is subsumed by the pursuit of economic value that dictates the labor process as a whole. Under capitalism, as Marx tells us in the *Grundrisse*, "[t]he social character of activities, as well as the social form of the product, and the share of individuals in production...appears as something alien and objective."[2] In *Capital* too, it is clear that Marx is concerned with unmasking the inversion of subject and object: the objectification of human capacity in alienated labor that denies the need for universality and also for the free association of that labor.

Much has been written in post-Marx Marxism that obscures the elementary fact that Marx's concern with social being is related to the concern over freedom and the reconstitution of human wholeness on an elevated level. While this is so, Dunayevskaya, one of the most perceptive of Marx's heirs, identified the humanist thread early on. Her Marxist-Humanism pushed to the fore the *human* categories in Marxism, so often obscured in economistic, not to mention structuralist and post-structuralist renderings. Dunayevskaya's

---

2. Marx, Karl (1993). *Grundrisse: Foundations of the Critique of Political Economy*, London: Penguin, p. 157.

incisive grasp of the *humanist essence of Marx* stands in full opposition to that of the anti-humanist thinkers who influence so much of the mainstream intellectual Left today, whether it be Michel Foucault, Louis Althusser, or Giorgio Agamben, among others. Particularly important, given his "Marxist" status, is Louis Althusser, whose thought is nonetheless implicated in the development of what are, in large part, strikingly *non*-Marxian forms of critique. Wholly at variance with Dunayevskaya's faithful and insightful reproduction of Marx, Althusser shoehorns Marx's project into a markedly objectivist "science of history" in which individuals are reduced to mere "supports" (*Träger*) in the division of labor, in the different levels of the structure.[3] This fantastic corruption of Marx, in which history is rendered as a *process without a subject*, reduces the subjectivity of individuals (*all* individuals) to that which is constructed in ideology: which is to say, hardly a subjectivity at all! As Dunayevskaya points out, this runs wholly contrary to Marx's own approach, which, despite the pages written on the fetishism of commodities and the reified consciousness that goes with it, nevertheless accords a central role to the self-activity of the proletariat (and other groups) in struggling for freedom.

Humanism as Praxis

For Dunayevskaya, then, as for Marx, and for us today, the humanism of Marx is neither a static nor an abstract humanism, but one directed toward to human agency, subjectivity, and to the unity of (and the *active act* of uniting) idealism and materialism in the social forces of the time. Responding to Marx's somewhat infamous statement that "[i]t is not the consciousness of men that determines their existence, but, on the contrary, their social existence that determines their consciousness" Dunayevskaya saw that "[t]here is nothing mechanical about this materialist conception of history: the *truth* that social existence determines consciousness is not a

---

3. Althusser, Louis & Balibar, Etienne (1970). *Reading Capital*, New York: New Left Books, p. 112.

confining wall, but a doorway to the future, as well as an appreciation of the past, of how men [sic] molded history."⁴ Marxist-Humanism is *both* a practical and a theoretical humanism; it is the *unity* of each, geared toward expressing, affirming, and encouraging the human capacity for realizing liberation in the world at large. Because of this, Marxist-Humanism avoids the twin pitfalls of *deterministic optimism* and *deterministic pessimism* – each the mirror image of the other, united together in both the history and the present of the Left.

Dunayevskaya recognized that Marx saw nothing "automatic" in the realization of socialism; it all depended on "the human subject, on the revolutionary compulsions of the proletariat to transform reality by undermining the existing order and creating a new one."⁵ Marxist-Humanism, facing towards praxis, doesn't sunder the human subject at the altar of the rarified theorist. The key relationship lies in *the connection between theory and practice*, which Marxist-Humanists view as a dialectical movement from practice to theory and from theory back to practice – not a closure but an opening, the key to which lies with "the *masses in motion* [and] not individual genius."⁶ Dunayevskaya was justifiably sharp in her criticism of the "professional Marxists" who operate with "too sophisticated an attitude to the revolts which have raged throughout the history of capitalism."⁷ "No theoretician," she tells us, "today more than ever before, can write out of his [sic] own head. Theory requires a *constant shaping and reshaping of ideas* on the basis of what the workers themselves are doing and thinking."⁸

Contrary to this approach, Dunayevskaya embodies the engaged practical thinker, concerned as was Marx with the need to transcend both in principle and in fact "the most monstrous" division of all: that between mental and manual labor. But while Marxist-Humanist theory doesn't come from above, practice should not be disconnected

---

4. Dunayevskaya, Raya (1973). *Philosophy and Revolution: From Hegel to Sartre, and from Marx to Mao*, New York: Delta, p. 153.

5. Ibid, p. 154.

6. Ibid.

7. Dunayevskaya, Raya (2000). *Marxism and Freedom: From 1776 until Today*, New York: Humanity Books, p. 116.

8. Ibid, p. 24, emphasis is mine.

from theory. As Dunayevskaya herself was quick to point out, "[a] ctivists by themselves are as one-sided as theory by itself. Only *in their unity* – in *a new relationship* that is rooted where the action is – can we rise to the challenge of the times."[9] In this stress on the importance of theory, Dunayevskaya openly set her position in opposition not only to her erstwhile colleagues, C. L. R. James and Grace Lee, but also to that of many anarchist and Maoist groupings, who either hold an instrumental relationship toward theory (in which it plays a only rudimentary role) or think that it could be picked up "en route" (which is tantamount to having no relationship with theory at all). Her engagement with theory – which for her *was* a form of practice – was inextricably connected to the making of history. This needs to be remembered not only in moments of seeming decline in the relations of struggle but also at the very height of insurrection.

Marxist-Humanism and the Expansion of the Dialectic

The notion of the "new passions and new forces" that Dunayevskaya enunciated on numerous occasions, and that is so central to Marxist-Humanism, comes originally from Chapter 32 of *Capital*, where Marx discusses his dialectical account of history as applied to the issue of accumulation. What Dunayevskaya is able to do in taking over the phrase is, through a reading which brings the "margins" of Marx to the very center, to *expand* the dialectic (in a way consistent with the late Marx himself) to Black and women's struggle (she also adds youth) as self-constituting elements in the progress of struggle. In this way, Dunayevskaya not only constitutes Marxist-Humanism as tied intensely to the present moment, to what is happening on the ground, but also, in fact, as futuristic, literally ahead of its time, and uniquely apposite to our own present moment.

This expanded conception of the dialectic – alive and connected as part of the wider striving for self-realization – is also important in

---

9. Dunayevskaya, Raya & Philips, Andy (1984). *A 1980s View: The Coal Miners' General Strike of 1949–50 and the Birth of Marxist Humanism*, Chicago: News & Letters, p. 41, emphasis is mine.

virtue of the fact that it counteracts the pessimism and melancholy of the intellectual and reformist Left. In the manner of the true humanism that Marx himself exhibited, Marxist-Humanism is a praxis *wholly open to the world*, to what is happening wherever it is happening, and is thereby global in a genuine sense. As Dunayevskaya was to remark toward the end of her life: "[w]hen a new revolution erupts, the tendency is to immediately try to box it in as if it were a question of France/Algeria; or of the West in general/the African revolutions; or in the Middle East, of Arab/Israel."[10] This "confining of the new within old categories"[11] represented a significant conceptual problem for Marxism, according to Dunayevskaya. As she astutely observes, pointing to what is essentially a narcissistically narrow view of the world, "[p]ost-Marx Marxists have disregarded too many revolutions, successful or aborted; disregarded too many philosophies underlying those revolutions. They just allow intellectual sloth to accumulate and accumulate."[12]

The importance of Dunayevskaya's notion of the Black masses as vanguard, then, the Black dimension that stands before us today (as do the women's dimension, and other dimensions), can hardly be overstated. What is clear is that the self-activity of the Black masses, and masses of all colors, are to the fore, demanding their freedom and giving succor to the notion of a *living, connected dialectic* – one that is contagious and increasingly global. This self-activity – which is also self-development and self-movement – has opened the fissures once again, and the pulse of insurrection beats faster. When Dunayevskaya defends production as her "point of departure... because to see the crisis in production is to understand it everywhere else,"[13] she is not giving the green light to economic or class reductionism. Whether the struggle concerns issues of class, race, gender, or sexuality, etc., or a combination of these aspects, the

---

10. Dunayevskaya, Raya (1986). *The Myriad Global Crises of the 1980s and the Nuclear War World since World War II*, Chicago: News & Letters, p. 20.

11. Ibid, pp. 20-1.

12. Ibid, p. 20.

13. Dunayevskaya, Raya (2000). *Marxism and Freedom: From 1776 until Today*, New York: Humanity Books, pp. 281-2.

dialectic between universal and particular is never sundered in an exclusionary concern for the one over the other. In as much as we are speaking of humanist struggles for self-realization – struggles pushing back against domination and fighting for the expansion of the space for freedom and self-realization at all levels of society – we aspire to struggles that are *connected and mutually interrogative*, possessing the potential to lead to the kind of progression that would usher in a real humanism instantiated in both production *and* social relations.

What is revealed here is humanism as a form of what Gramsci called "absolute humanism," which for Dunayevskaya is nothing other than "the articulation needed to sum up a class*less*, *non*-racist, *non*-sexist society, where truly new human relations self-develop."[14]

Marxist-Humanism in the Heat of the Present

As we stand in the heat of the present, not only does the *need* for Marxist-Humanism shout out to us through the tear gas that shrouds our city streets; moreover, the *power* of Marxist-Humanism to grasp the human expression of the need for universality, and to account for the articulation of this need in the present, as what promises to be a *turning-point* in the battles against our dehumanized reality, is unrivalled. When Dunayevskaya speaks of the "new passions and new forces" erupting in society, she speaks not only of the sense in which the dialectic has been broadened to include the Black, women's, and youth dimensions; she also speaks to the fact that *the process of the dialectic* is never fully pushed underground, even at moments when the foreclosure of history seems to have descended upon us. In highlighting this fact of the dialectic, the *humanism* of Marxist-Humanism demonstrates its superiority – intellectual and practical – to those abstract anti-humanist intellectuals of which we have already spoken.

Take, for example, Agamben's recent fears that the emergency measures taken against COVID-19 would lead to the pacification

---

14. Dunayevskaya, Raya "Intellectuals in the Age of State Capitalism" in (ed.) Hudis, Peter (1992). *The Marxist Humanist Theory of State Capitalism: Selected Writings*, Chicago: News & Letters, p. 11.

of politics. Railing against the "supposed epidemic of coronavirus," the performative contradiction that blights every anti-humanist account of the social rears its head also in Agamben's most recent pronouncements. "People have been so habituated to live in conditions of perennial crisis and perennial emergency" he tells us, "that they don't seem to notice that their life has been reduced to a purely biological condition and has not only every social and political dimension, but also human and affective." While it is certainly the case that we are witness, alongside and in intimate relation to the protests, to a vicious crackdown and a reactionary tightening of legislation that will enshrine outright fascist control of dissent (what else can we call the labelling of Antifa as a "terrorist organization"?!), the insurrection that has broken out has only confirmed as woefully undialectical the anti-humanism that reduces individuals to subjects (in the singular sense) that are *acted upon*. While it is true that what we have seen in the recent weeks is the extension to even white protestors of the localized and normalized "state of exception" that exists in relation to the Black people and people of colour in the U.S. (and elsewhere), the rising to consciousness and action of thousands upon thousands has given the lie to the anti-humanist pretence at radicality.

The focus on the pacification of individuals, characteristic of Agamben, as it is Foucault, Adorno, Althusser, etc., *has been blown out of the water* in response to yet another brutal murder of a Black man. Although Agamben is right to say that "[a] society that lives in a perennial state of emergency cannot be a free society," it is simply not the case, as he suggests, that "our society no longer believes in anything but *bare life*" (emphasis is mine). What are the recent protests – protests that have spread all over the world, and that have moved beyond supposedly particularistic concerns – other than an affirmation of a life lived without fear of death and brutalization, and one pushing for something *more than* bare subsistence? Thousands are literally putting their lives on the line in order to bring about a state of affairs where people of color no longer have to live in fear of their own life, and in which the related and equally life-denying structures of capitalism are increasingly called into question. It's hard to see how a focus on the "biopolitics" of the state, as found in Agamben and Foucault, can account for the degree of recalcitrance and the development of consciousness that seems to be coalescing in the present.

In the heat of this present, then, what stands out are the new passions and forces that have *spontaneously* come to the fore. The vitality of the Marxist-Humanist view – of the inviolability of human subjectivity, human resistance, human consciousness – takes on a marked importance as we face the specter of a new Great Depression and the related heightening of repressive forces. During a period in which the pressure of the routinised extraction of surplus value has been temporarily thrown off for millions (who are also walking a tightrope of survival), the white heat of the present is not likely to be dampened over what promises to be months upon months. What is less certain is the future of the insurrection: whether it can sustain itself and transcend to a higher level. What was marked out as crucial by Dunayevskaya in such a movement from practice that has disclosed its quest for universality is that, for the turning point to be realized, "theory and practice [need to] finally evolve a unified organizational form."[15] Organization, as the realization of praxis, is imperative, but it cannot be an organization in the Bolshevik sense of the Vanguard Party.

To where, then, do we turn? What is certain is that the organizational form must have *humanism* as central to its functioning: it must be a system through which human value is not only valorized but affirmed in practice. The coalescence of objective and subjective forces in the developed consciousness – i.e. praxis – of our age is the ground from which these considerations must flow. But the new passions and forces need to be melded to *a theory* – Marxist-Humanism – that both arises from them and returns to them. As Dunayevskaya put it in *Philosophy and Revolution*:

> No new stage of cognition is born out of thin air. It can be born only out of *praxis*. When workers are ready for a new plunge to freedom, that is when we reach also a new stage of cognition... The masses have shown how different proletarian "subjectivity" is from petty-bourgeois subjectivity. They refuse any longer to be only the force of revolution, for they are also

---

15. Dunayevskaya, Raya (1983). *American Civilization on Trial: Black Masses as Vanguard*, Chicago: News & Letters, p. 34.

its reason, active participants in working out the philosophy of liberation for our age. They have begun. Is it now the time for intellectuals to begin, with where the workers are and what they think, to fill the theoretic void in the Marxist movement.[16]

---

16. Dunayevskaya, Raya (1973). *Philosophy and Revolution: From Hegel to Sartre, and Marx to Mao*, New York: Delta, pp. 265–6.

Chapter 8

Toward the Unification of Theory and Practice in the International Marxist-Humanist Organization

By Jens Johansson

Discusses challenges, possibilities, and future aims for the IMHO as an organization. Adapted from an organizational report delivered to the 2020 Convention of the International Marxist-Humanist Organization in July.

This paper will focus not on the objective development of capitalism, nor on the development of the mass movements, but rather on the subjective development of IMHO as an organization. However, I will still start by pointing out an important development in the consciousness of the mass movements. This is because I believe it will have an impact on the future of our work.

The point I want to emphasize is that the Black Lives Matter movement, which has been very active these last weeks by protesting police abuse against Blacks and mass incarceration in America, is not only a US-movement, but an international movement. Much in thanks to the new communication technologies, the protestors are in very close contact with other protestors around the world. They are exchanging experiences in order to not only show international solidarity, but also to learn from each other and to understand how issues in one corner of the globe can illuminate the essence of an issue in another corner. But the attempts to connect and to understand the essence of the problems doesn't stop there. Remember that many of the Black Lives Matter activists who are out protesting today were also out protesting the destruction of the climate and Indigenous rights less than a year ago, and many were also out protesting against sexism during the #MeToo-movement a while before that. Thus, the attempts of today's activists to connect and understand the essence of the problem are made not only internationally, around the globe, but also interdimensionally, with different freedom struggles.

Nonetheless, while these international and interdimensional connections are absolutely crucial and extremely important, I am not sure that we can claim that there are specific characteristics of the movement that the generation of activists today make up. But one thing I do believe that we can claim is a new and original contribution that this generation has developed very far is the consciousness about anti-racism, about inclusion, care of each other, representation of all races and sexes, consciousness about one's positionality, that everyone should have the possibility to speak and to be heard, and cognizance of the symbolic violence objectified in language, symbols, and statues, etc. This consciousness is something that I don't think any previous generation has been so good at developing as today's generation. In concrete terms, this is a consciousness that pushes forth a more human and inclusive environment. Therefore, it is something that should not be dismissed or ridiculed, but instead something that also the IMHO can develop from by embracing and learning from. What it basically comes down to is that it is an acknowledgement of experiences of marginalization and a recognition of the human reaction to practices of social exclusion and stratification.

Developing a Theory of Liberation

The first sentence in our constitution reads, "The International Marxist-Humanist Organization (IMHO) aims to develop and project a viable vision of an alternative to capitalism – a new, human society – that can give direction to today's freedom struggles." This sentence, I believe, encapsulates the whole purpose of the existence of our organization. The question, then, that we in the IMHO need to try to work out an answer to is: how does one develop and how does one project a viable vision of an alternative to capitalism?

Hegel spent a lot of time critiquing his friend Schelling for jumping over the particular when they discussed the absolute idea. Hegel complained that Schelling thought that he could arrive at the absolute idea by skipping over the particular, thus to arrive at the absolute like a "shot-out-of-a-pistol." The problem with that, Hegel thought, was that Schelling's absolute idea then had no connection to reality. Schelling's absolute idea was therefore running the risk of becoming completely abstract. Instead, Hegel meant that in order to reach the absolute, one has to approach it via the particular. This is so, because Hegel argued that the essence of an object must appear for us in a particular form. He meant that there can't be an impassable barrier between the essence of an object and how that same object appears for us. Instead, he thought that an aspect of the essence must appear in a particular form in the world of appearances.

This is an important idea for us when we try to develop a viable alternative to capitalism. It is important because it means that when we start theorizing about what an alternative might be, we need to begin by grounding our analysis in the concrete particular experiences of daily life that people live today, in their specific contexts. With that in mind, where should we stand? We need to ask, "What problems exists out there?" We then need to listen to what those who are the most oppressed say. And what do they say? Well, today they are coming out to the streets and are literally shouting about stopping police violence against Black people. Our task as members of the IMHO is then to grasp those experiences and to go beyond the surface manifestation to try to understand what those experiences in the world of appearances are expressions of. To that end, what is the essence of what we see? When we have reached the essence, what we do then is start formulating a notion of an alternative out of a philosophy of revolution based on Marx's humanism. It is here that we as subjects starts to appear because it is here that we define what a new society could be like and, thus, also what we as human beings could be like in this new society. This, beginning in the particular experiences of today, is what is meant by grounding the theory in the concrete. Because the particularities always change, every new generation has to work out a theory of liberation anew.

Projecting a Theory of Liberation

Trying to connect different freedom movements with a revolutionary philosophy based on Marx's humanism was indeed what Dunayevskaya tried to do when the whole development of Marxist-Humanism, as we know it today, once begun.

There are thousands of great examples of how she did this, but just to pick one which I think also speaks to today, I would lift up an article which she wrote in 1944 entitled Marxism and the Negro Problem. In this piece, Dunayevskaya emphasizes the independent validity of the anti-racist struggle, apart from the class struggle. Moreover, in it, she also addresses the specific realities facing Blacks. No Marxist in the United States had said anything like that before she and the others in the Johnson-Forest Tendency said so. In one section of the article she writes:

> Historians who state that the Negro problem is rooted in slavery and stop there fail to see the crux of the question. The "stigma" of slavery could not have persisted so long if the economic remains of slavery had not persisted. The Civil War abolished the institutions of slavery, but did not give the land to him who tilled it. Not having got the land, the peasant's fate was inevitable, whether he be white or Negro. Even in Russia, where there was some fraudulent attempt to give the serf the land, it was impossible for the Russian serf to rise above the needs of the backward economy. All the more so in the South where the Negro did not get his "40 acres and a mule". Cotton remaining dominant, semifeudal relationships were inevitable. The division of labor set up by the cotton economy may not be disturbed. The social relations arising on the basis of the cotton economy remain "less changed than the soil itself on which the cotton is grown". Within the economic remains of slavery lie the economic roots of the Negro Question.[1]

Furthermore, in the same article she also says that even if the Black people's movement develops in a reactionary way, and even if the revolutionary Marxists are unable to influence the movement, that only proves that Marxists needs to go even further in their

---

1. Dunayevskaya, Raya "Marxism and the Negro Problem: A Discussion Article", June 18, 1944, p. 264. Accessible here: https://rayadunayevskaya.org/ArchivePDFs/259.pdf

attempt to understand the underlying, deep economic and social causes giving rise to the development. The completely wrong way to engage the Black people's movement, she writes, is to dismiss the movement and throw epithets at it (here one can think of those who dismiss today's anti-racist movement by putting epithets like "criminals" or "looters" on it).

But how does this example from Dunayevskaya actually help us to figure out the role of the IMHO today? I believe that in one sense we could say that the role of IMHO is a counter position of Lenin and Trotsky's idea of the vanguard party. Lenin had the idea that, not just the revolutionary organization, but also the revolutionary theory should come from the vanguard party, which was to consist of a group of intellectuals who would know what is to be done. Dunayevskaya broke with that idea in the 1940s, and the IMHO has not turned back to it since. Instead, we strongly oppose the idea of a vanguard party that leads the masses, and we oppose the thought that revolutionary theory should come from an outside group disconnected from the masses.

However, we do not oppose the need for organizations as such which can make a contribution to today's new movements by addressing the question of an alternative to capitalism. C. L. R. James held a view that spontaneous mass movements already contain within them the complete answer to what the new society is. Thus, he did not see the need for an organization that can help articulate that idea. IMHO today does not oppose James's emphasis on spontaneous movements; we emphasize them as well, but on the contrary, we do see a need for an organization.

Dunayevskaya position on this was that revolutionary consciousness, and even some forms of revolutionary theory, emerge from the oppressed in response to an array of material conditions, but that such revolutionary consciousness is not reducible to revolutionary theory. Instead, she meant that revolutionary philosophy has to be worked out by hard conceptual labor on the part of the intellectuals, as well as the masses, and that some hard theoretical and philosophical labor is needed to get there.

I believe that the specific importance that the IMHO has in relation to today's new movement is to address and project the question of alternatives to capitalism. That is because we have a body of ideas that fit very well to address this question. Thanks to our rich ideas of Marxism and of humanism (not liberal or Enlightenment humanism, but revolutionary dialectical humanism), we can discuss not only what we are against, but also what we are for. What we are for is a new form of universal humanism which unifies the alienated human being.

Today, truckloads of people are coming out to demonstrations. More and more of those are interested in alternatives to capitalism and are looking for groups that have something to offer in the way of that. The question, then, is if the IMHO will be there and make a humanist alternative available, or if it will only be other groups out there talking about some kind of redistribution model, or more authoritarian variants, as the alternative to capitalism?

References

Agambem, G. (2020, February 26). The Invention of an Epidemic. *Quodlibet.*

Agamben, G. (2020, March 17). Clarifications. *An und für sich.*

Aljairi, J., Majed, R., & Achcar, G. (2020, January 21). *Special Panel Event: The Second Arab Spring: Seasons of Revolution.* SOAS, Univeristy of London, London.

Althusser, L., & Etienne, B. (1970). *Reading Capital.* New York: New Left Books.

Anderson, K. B., & Rockwell, R. (Eds.). (2012). *The Dunayevskaya-Marcuse-Fromm Correspondence, 1954-1978: Dialogues on Hegel, Marx and Critical Theory.* Maryland: Lexington Books.

Andrew, S. (2020, May 19). Covid-19 Lockdowns Could Drop Carbon Emissions to Their Lowest Since World War II, but the Change May be Temporary. *CNN.*

Battacharya, T. (2017). *Social Reproduction Theory: Remapping Class, Recentering Oppression.* London: Pluto Press.

Boccacci, J. M. (2020, February 3). Citizen Assemblies Are Challenging the Neoliberal Model in Chile. *Orinoca Tribune.*

Brennan, M. (2020, August 12). Amid Pandemic, Confidence in Key U.S. Institutions Surges. *Gallup.*

Carver, T. (1996). *Marx: Later Political Writings.* Cambridge: Cambridge University Press.

Casey, R. (2020, March 17). Does Florida Really Want Ex-Felons to Vote? *The New York Times.*

Chen, T. (2017, January 23). People Have Strong Feelings About Cops High-Fiving People in the Women's March in Atlanta. *Buzzfeed.*

Choudry, A., & Vally, S. (2018). *Reflections on Knowledge, Learning and Social Movements: History's Schools.* New York: Routledge.

Crabtree, S. (2020, July 22). Most Americans Say Policing Needs 'Major Changes'. *Gallup.*

DeSantis, R. (2020, June 11). Navajo Nation Has More COVID-19 Cases Than 12 States - and More Deaths Than 7 States Combined. *People.*

Douthat, R. (2020, February 9). The Age of Decadence. *The New York Times.*

Duda, J. (2017, November 9). Towards the horizon of abolition: A conversation with Mariam. *The Next System Project.*

Dunayevskaya, R. (1944, June 18). *Marxism and the Negro Problem: A Discussion Article.* Retrieved from The Raya Dunayevskaya Collection: Marxist-Humanist Archives: https://rayadunayevskaya.org/ArchivePDFs/259.pdf

Dunayevskaya, R. (1981). *Rosa Luxemburg, Women's Liberation, and Marx's Philosophy of Revolution.* New Jersey: Humanities Press.

Dunayevskaya, R. (1982). *Rosa Luxemburg, Women's Liberation and Marx's Philosophy of Revolution.* Urbana: University of Illinois.

Dunayevskaya, R. (1983). *American Civilization on Trial: Black Masses as Vanguard*. Chicago: News & Letters.

Dunayevskaya, R. (1986). *The Myriad Global Crises of the 1980s and the Nuclear War World since World War II*. Chicago: News & Letters.

Dunayevskaya, R. (2000). *Marxism and Freedom: From 1776 until Today*. New York: Humanity Books.

Dunayevskaya, R. (2015). *Philosophy and Revolution: From Hegel to Sartre, and from Marx to Mao*. Delhi: Aakar Books.

Dunayevskaya, R. (2015). *Rosa Luxemburg, Women's Liberation and Marx's Philosophy of Revolution*. Delhi: Aakar Books.

Dunayevskaya, R., & Philips, A. (1984). *A 1980s View: The Coal Miners' General Strike of 1949-50 and the Birth of Marxist Humanism*. Chicago: News & Letters.

Fanon, F. (1973). *The Wretched of the Earth*. New York: Penguin.

Fanon, F. (2018). *Alienation and Freedom*. London: Bloomsbury.

Ferguson, S. (2020). *Women and Work: Feminism, Labour, and Social Reproduction*. London: Pluto Press.

Fromm, E. (2004). *Marx's Concept of Man*. New York: Continuum.

Goldberg, M. (2020, May 19). *The Phony Class War*. The New York Times.

Grabar, H. (2019, Janaury 25). What Workers Can Learn From 'the Largest Lockout in U.S. History. *Slate*.

Hägglund, M. (2020). *This Life: Secular Faith and Spiritual Freedom*. New York: Pantheon.

Hathaway, B. (2020, May 19). New analysis quantifies risk of COVID-19 to racial, ethnic minorities. *Yale News*.

Hudis, P. (Ed.). (1992). *The Marxist-Humanist Theory of State Capitalism*. Chicago: News & Letters.

Hudis, P. (2012). *Marx's Concept of the Alternative to Capitalism*. Chicago: Haymarket.

Hudis, P. (2019, April). How is an Intersectional Historical Materialism Possible?: The Dialectic of Race and Class Reconsidered. *Historical Materialism*. Toronto.

Hudis, P., & Le Blanc, P. (Eds.). (2016). *The Complete Works of Rosa Luxemburg: Economic Writings (Vol. 2)*. Brooklyn: Verso.

Johansson, J., Anderson, K. B., Monzó, L. D., Ludenhoff, K., & Hudis, P. (2020, April 10). Where to Begin? Growing Seeds of Liberation in a World Torn Asunder. *The International Marxist-Humanist*.

Kaplan, E., & Davis, T. (2020, May 30). Huge Dispararity in COVID-19 death rates for Native Americans in NM. *Albuquerque Journal*.

Kitonga, N. (2020, June 13). Black Lives Matter Uprising in Los Angeles: Working Toward a New Humanist Society. *The International Marxist-Humanist*.

Krieger, N. (2015, January). Trends in US deaths due to legal intervention among black and white men, age 15-34 years, by county income level: 1960-2010. *Harvard Public Health Review, Vol. 3.*

Langer Research Associates. (2020, July 21). 63 Percent Support Black Lives Matter as Recognition of Discrimination Jumps. *Langer Research.*

Lober, B. (2018, January). "(re)Thinking Sex Positivity, Abolition Feminism, and the #MeToo Movement: Opportunity for a New Synthesis. *Abolition: A Journal of Insurgent Politics.*

Loewus, L. (2017, August 15). The Nation's Teaching Force Is Still Mostly White and Female. *Education Week.*

Mansfield, M. (2018, June 13). What is Abolitionist Feminism, and Why Does it Matter? *The Progressive Policy Think Tank.*

Marx, K. (1976). *Capital: A Critique of Political Economy (Vol. 1).* New York: Penguin.

Marx, K. (1973). *Grundrisse: Foundations of the Critique of Political Economy.* New York: Penguin.

Marx, K. (1974). *Ethnological Notebooks.* Assen: Van Gorcum.

Marx, K., & Engels, F. (1975). *Marx-Engels Collected Works (Vol. 3).* New York: International Publishers.

Marx, K., & Engels, F. (1986). *Marx-Engels Collected Works (Vol. 22).* London: Lawrence & Wishart.

McFarquhar, N. (2020, May 16). Workers in Stores, Already at Risk, Confront Violence When Enforcing Mask Rules. *The New York Times.*

McKittrick, K. (Ed.). (2015). *Sylvia Wynter: On Being Human as Praxis.* Durham: Duke Univeristy Press.

Monzó, L. D. (2019). *A Revolutionary Subject: Pedagogy of Women of Color and Indigeneity.* New York: Peter Lang.

Monzó, L. D., & McLaren, P. (2017, December 18). Red Love: Toward Racial, Economic and Social Justice. *Truthout.*

Moore, J. W. (2015). *Capitalism and the Web of Life: Ecology and the Accumulation of Capital.* New York: Verso.

Oluo, I. (2017, March 24). Women of Color Assess the Impact of the Women's March. *Here & Now.*

Osterweil, V. (2014, August 21). In Defense of Looting. *New Inquiry.*

Oxfam International. (2020, June 1). *Extreme Inequality and Essential Services.* Retrieved from Oxfam International: https://www.oxfam.org/en/what-we-do/issues/extreme-inequality-and-essential-services

Parivartan ki Disha. (2020, February 23). Citizenship Amendment Act (CAA) and National Register for Citizens (NRC) are violent attacks against the working and oppressed masses of India. *The International Marxist-Humanist.*

Patel, R., & Moore, J. W. (2017). *A History of the World in Seven Cheap Things: A Guide to Capitalism*, Nature, and the Future of the Planet. Berkeley: University of California Press.

Ramirez, R. (2020, May 4). A Tale of Two Crises: Wake-Up Call: As coronavirus ravages Louisiana, 'cancer alley' residents haven't given up the fight against polluters. *Grist*.

Ramirez, R. (2020, January 15). Another legacy of redlining: Unequal exposure to heat waves. *Grist*.

Regan, H. (2020, May 6). Billions of People Could Live in Areas Too Hot for Humans by 2070, Study Says. *CNN*.

Rice, D. (2019, March 12). Study Finds Race Gap in Air Pollution - Whitess Largely Cause It, Blacks and Hispanics Breath It. *USA Today*.

Roberts, M. (2020, February 2). *Trump's Trickle Dries Up*. Retrieved from Michael Roberts Blog: https://thenextrecession.wordpress.com/2020/02/04/trumps-trickle-dries-up/

Rowlatt, J. (2020, June 20). Greta Thunberg: Climate Change 'As Urgent' as Coronavirus. *BBC*.

Roy, A. (2020, April 3). The pandemic is a portal. *Financial Times*.

Ruas, R. (2019, August 31). The Amazon Burns and the Politics of Death: Resisting the Commodification of Our Future. *The International Marxist-Humanist*.

Ruas, R. (2020). A crise desvelamento das dinamicas de producao da vida no capitalismo: um comentario a Tithi Battacharya. In G. Goncalves, *Covid-19, Capitalismo e Crise: bibliografia comentada* (pp. 180-90). Rio de Janeiro: LEICC e Revista Direito e Praxis.

Ruoshui, W. (1985). A Defense of Humanism. *Chinese Studies in Philosophy*, Vol. 16:3, pp. 71-88.

Saito, K. (2017). Marx in Anthropocene: Value, Metabolic Rift, and the Non-Cartesian Dualism. *Zeitschrift für kritische Sozialtheorie*, 4(1-2), pp. 276-95.

Samudzi, Z. (2020, May 16). White Witness and the Contemporary Lynching. *The New Republic*.

Shah, S. (2016). *Pandemic: Tracking Contagions from Cholera to Ebola and Beyond*. New York: Sarah Crichton Books, Farrar, Straus, and Giroux.

Shahin, T. (1983). *Late Marx and the Russian Road*. New York: Monthly Review Press Classics.

Smialek, J. (2020, March 24). The Fed Plans to Do Whatever It Takes, and More than It Ever Has. *The New York Times*, B4-5.

Smulewicz-Zucker, G., & Thompson, M. J. (Eds.). (2020). *An Inheritance for Our Times: The Principles and Politics of Democratic Socialism*. New York: OR Books.

Stevenson, A., & Wang, V. (2020, June 4). Why China May Call the World's Bluff on Hong Kong. *The New York Times*.

Tartaglia, L. (2020, March 20). Dispatch from Italy: Class Struggle in the Time of Coronavirus. *Labor Notes*.

Taylor, K.-Y. (2016). From *#BlackLivesMatter to Black Liberation*. Chicago: Haymarket.

Taylor, K.-Y. (2020, August 14). We should still defund the police. *The New Yorker*.

Vogel, L. (2013). *Marxism and the Oppression of Women: Toward a Unitary Theory*. Chicago: Haymarket Books.

Wright, R. (2019, December 30). The Story of 2019: Protests in Every Corner of the Globe. *The New Yorker*.